OF WALKING BEAMS AND PADDLE WHEELS

A white-woven web of staunch steel against a spring sky, the mighty walking beam, symbol of the ferryboat, rises loftily to drive its companion worker, the paddle wheel, as they team up for the conquest of San Francisco Bay.

OF

WALKING BEAMS
AND
PADDLE WHEELS

A CHRONICLE OF
SAN FRANCISCO BAY FERRYBOATS

BY
GEORGE H. HARLAN
AND
CLEMENT FISHER JR

BAY BOOKS
LIMITED
742 MARKET ST.
SAN FRANCISCO, CALIF.

LITHOGRAPHED BY

EL Camino PRESS

SALINAS, CALIFORNIA

Gratefully Dedicated To
Honorary Captains of The
San Francisco Bay Ferries

HERB CAEN

SAMUEL DICKINSON

THE LATE EARLE ENNIS

JERRY MC MULLIN

ROBERT O'BRIEN

And

Their Honorary First Officers,
The Former Ferryboat Commuters

HOIST THE GANGPLANK

**I**N A "LETTERS TO THE EDITOR" column in the local press, I recently read four words: "Ferry boats are obsolete" — and I shivered. They were such dismal, tragic words. Like saying an old race horse is obsolete. Or an old lady and an old gentleman are obsolete. Almost like saying that sentiment is obsolete. And I have always been sentimental about the ferryboats that plied the waters of San Francisco Bay.

My first memory of them is a nebulous thing; it was not so much the boat itself as the end it achieved that made such a confused, cacophonous, and yet lasting impression on my child-mind. There was the rush across the deck as the boat edged into the apron, the rush through the dark alleys of the old Ferry Building, and then the sudden erupting into the hysterical din of lower Market Street, and out of that overwhelming noise, only one sound became articulate — I still can hear it after more than fifty years have passed: The cries of the cabbies, and hack drivers, and bus drivers, shouting: "Russ House! Russ House!" "Lick House! Lick House!" "The Cosmopolitan! Bus going right to the Cosmopolitan Hotel!"

That was when I was very young. In the years that followed there was another impression that was very much more tangible: The exultation I always experienced when, returning from a trip, I would stand on the forward upper deck of the ferry boat and see the city rising out of the Bay, gilded with the gold of the setting sun, or silvered with the grey of the phantom fog. Today I know that much of my love of San Francisco was born of those upper-deck views of the city. They, the busy, chattering, pompous, and for that matter, rather arrogant little ships, have always been a part of my love for San Francisco.

Busy, chattering, pompous, arrogant — and beautiful — the ferry boats were personalities, individuals, more like people than any other inanimate objects, as for that matter, are all ships and boats, and because they had so many human attributes, they deserved a biography. Here it is, then, the story of the life of the ferry boats: *Of Walking Beams & Paddle Wheels.* It is, as far as I know, the only book devoted entirely to the adventures, and industry, and romance and whims of the ferry boats of San Francisco Bay. Turning these pages, looking at the illustrations that have fascinated me as much as has the text of the book, I am reminded of the day that I crossed the Bay with a companion. I was going from Oakland High School with a basket containing twenty carrier pigeons that I planned to release on the brink of Russian Hill and watch them wing their way back across the Bay to our Fruitvale home. My companion, a casual acquaintance who had gone to Oakland High School a few years before me, was Jack London. We stood up there on the upper forward deck, watching the city come out of a heavy morning fog, and suddenly an eastbound ferry boat crossed our bow, bellowing its warning in a great little voice. And Jack London said: "The silly old lady! That's what the ferry boats remind me of — little old Queen Victorias."

Look at the pictures in these pages and I think you'll see what Jack London meant. But of course, the pictures, fascinating as they are, comprise only a small part of this book, if not in space surely in importance. The ferry boats were so much a part of the history of the city's first hundred years, that their story becomes the story of San Francisco and the Bay Cities and that story, for students of history, is also here, carefully documented.

History? When Don Gaspar first saw the Bay from the skyline near the Creek of the Fleas, he gave up his expedition; the Bay separated the south from the north, an all but impassable Bay, by ferry boat, ever since A. A. Cohen built his first ferry boat in Alameda, that every westbound traveler came.

·Memory upon memory floods past, insistent, persistent, as I turn the pages. The days when we came rattling onto the deck of the *Solano,* the biggest ferry boat in the world, in the railway train that had brought us across the continent. The Sundays we crossed to Sausalito to wander up the pipe line out of Mill Valley, to West Point, and the crest of Tamalpais. And then the joyous return on the ferry boat, a noisy, hectic young crowd, most of us headed for North Beach and a fifty-cent Italian dinner with red wine. Then the . . . . .

But go ahead and read the book. To you, too, it will bring back memories, different than mine, perhaps; the same as mine, perhaps. The memories are there, in this story of the inanimate old things with human attributes, the ferry boats that plied the waters of San Francisco Bay.

SAMUEL DICKSON

Radio City
San Francisco 2, California
August 1, 1951

"CAST OFF!"

I T HAS BEEN more than ten years since the last of the commuter passenger ferry lines on San Francisco Bay was discontinued, and nearly a decade and a half has passed since the completion of the two mighty bridges which made further operation of most of the passenger and vehicular ferries unnecessary. The ferries have slowly been joining the ranks of the forgotten as their host of passengers have been absorbed largely by a class of bus riders and, in a lesser degree, by the interurban electric trains which now cross San Francisco Bay. Their combined numbers, strangely enough, never equalled in number and probably never will equal the great throng which rode — and loved — the ferries.

In the preface to *Oil Lamps & Iron Ponies*, the present co-authors referred to a second volume then in the planning. After the publication of the railroad book, the only one of its kind devoted exclusively to narrow-gauge railroads, so much interest was expressed in the portions of various of the chapters having to do with the ferries of San Francisco Bay that work on the second railroad book was deferred and all effort was concentrated on a volume devoted exclusively to the ferry lines. It is hoped by the authors that, in telling this story, they have filled a gap in the history of San Francisco Bay and its environs for never before has such a story been attempted, never before has such material been collected and compiled in a single volume.

It is not the purpose of this book to tell the complete history of all the ferry lines of San Francisco Bay nor to attempt a too detailed account of even the more important of them. Rather, a sincere and real effort has been made to "tell a tale," recreating the color and flavor of ferryboat days, at the same time recording at least a skeleton of facts and figures for future historians. While interlocking with the stories of the Bay ferryboats to some extent, the separate story of the sternwheel river boats has been reserved for another volume since theirs is equally as important in the over-all transportation picture as that of the ferries, the interurban railroads, and the mainline railroads.

The material of the authors has been generously augmented by that of the foremost collectors of data on inland waterway transportation on the Bay of San Francisco, former operators of the ferry lines, and the present owners of the remaining ferry systems. In many instances, the records are vague and only through the word-of-mouth reporting of former captains and engineers of the ferries has information been obtained. Company records as well as those of the Department of Commerce are very sketchy for the early days of operation. It is truly regretted that old ferries were not the subject of more records and writings than they appear to have been. Unfortunate, but all too true.

It is hoped that the reader of this volume may have made a ferry trip across the Bay at one time or another — one trip that stands out in his or her mind as a pleasant never-to-be-forgotten experience with the bright sun in a blue sky sparkling on the green salt water or perhaps the twinkling stars and crescent moon dancing in the murky water of the Bay. And if, in perusing one chapter or another, the memories of the ferry and the trip across the Bay are pleasantly and vividly recalled because of the refreshing incidents recounted hereafter, the authors of this work will feel that their efforts have been well expended and that still another purpose will have been well served.

GEORGE H. HARLAN
CLEMENT FISHER, JR.

San Francisco, California
1 May, 1951

ACKNOWLEDGMENTS

Few books have ever been written without a lot of assistance to the authors by those on the sidelines and in the background. In grateful acknowledgment of their many and varied contributions, then, the authors of the present work extend thanks to:

Mr. Robert W. Parkinson for historical data, source drawings, and general information;

Mr. Roy D. Graves for selected photographs and data;

Mr. C. Ferry Hatch for the records of the Monticello Steamship Company and the Golden Gate Ferry together with additional data and information;

Mr. Ray Clarke for data on the early history of the Richmond - San Rafael Ferry;

Mr. Emmett Fitzpatrick of the Southern Pacific Company for data and photographs;

Mr. Harold Burroughs of the Atchison, Topeka & Santa Fe Railway for data;

Mr. Gilbert Kneiss of the Western Pacific Railroad for photographs;

Commander Donald V. Reardon, Naval Architect, U.S.C.G., Twelfth Coast Guard District, Rear Admiral Joseph E. Sitka, Commander, for various mechanical records and data.

GEORGE H. HARLAN
CLEMENT FISHER, JR.

CONTENTS

■   ■

■ ■ ■

LIST OF PLATES

∎ ∎

I
Double-End Wooden Ferryboat *Newark* of the
South Pacific Coast Railroad
Facing Page 30

∎

II
Double-End Wooden Ferryboat *Sacramento* of the
Southern Pacific Railroad
Facing Page 42

∎

III
Typical Walking Beam Engine of a San Francisco Bay
Double-End Ferryboat
Facing Page 70

∎

IV
Midship Section of the Wooden Passenger Ferry *Tiburon*
Facing Page 81

∎

V
Single-End Wooden Ferryboat *James M. Donahue* of the
San Francisco & North Pacific Railroad
Facing Page 84

∎

VI
Double-End Wooden Ferryboat *Tiburon* of the
San Francisco & North Pacific Railroad
Facing Page 87

∎ ∎ ∎

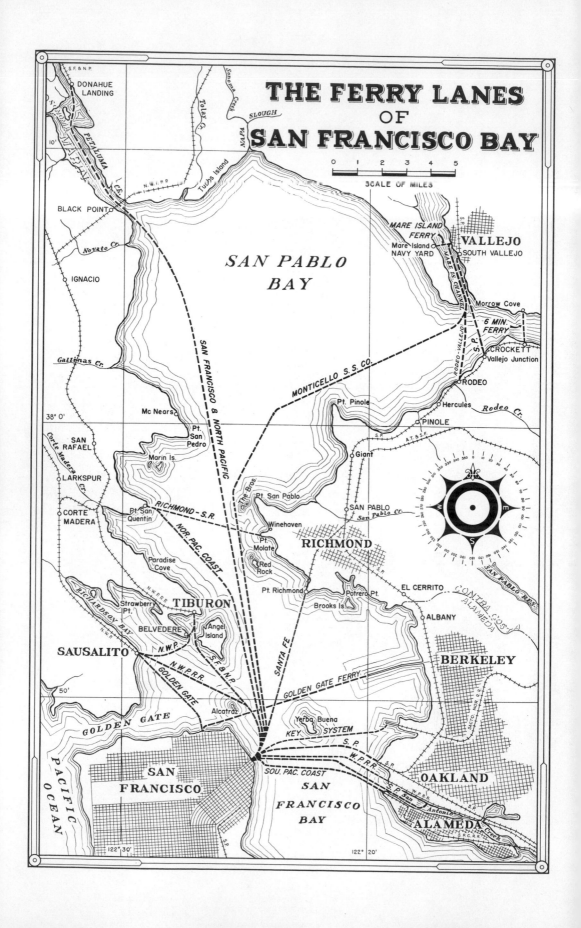

CHAPTER I

SALUTE TO THE FERRYBOAT

WHAT SAN FRANCISCO'S CABLE CARS are to the "City by the Golden Gate," so were the ferryboats of San Francisco Bay to Marin, Oakland, Berkeley, Richmond, Alameda, and all the other communities on the shores of the West's largest land-locked harbor. Certainly other cities have had their own ferry services — New York's huge web of transriver commuter boats, Chicago's ocean-going-sized lake steamers, San Diego's combination auto-and-passenger ferries to the Silver Strand of Coronado. But none of them possess the color, the romance, the universal appeal that belongs particularly to the ferryboats of San Francisco Bay. For almost a century, these vessels ploughed through storms and fogs to render a service so vital to the life and very existence of the grateful communities which patronized them.

It would be difficult to even estimate the number of persons who have traveled aboard the ferries, exclusive of the daily commuters from the North Shore, the East Shore, and from Alameda for, prior to 1936, when the San Francisco - Oakland Bay Bridge was opened to traffic, no one who arrived at Richmond, Metropolitan Oakland, or Alameda by way of the Santa Fe Railway, the Southern Pacific's Overland or Shasta routes, or the Western Pacific's Feather River route, could enter San Francisco save by ferry. Indeed, even to this day, there is no transcontinental train service directly into San Francisco, passengers having to change to a Southern Pacific ferry at Oakland Pier if arriving by Southern Pacific or Western Pacific, or to a motor coach at Fortieth and San Pablo Station if using the Grand Canyon Line of the "Atchison Topeka and the Santa Fe."

But it was not these very welcome cross-country visitors that created the legend and the lore of the walking-beamed and paddle-wheeled vessels which majestically and serenely sailed through the blue waters of San Francisco Bay but rather the thousands of commuters who "twice a day crossed the Bay." And the churning of paddle wheels was as continuous and familiar a sight on the city's waterfront as the clang of the fog bell or the blare of the warning klaxon at the end of the Ferry Building's middle ferry slip, for the ferry lanes were numerous and their followers were frequent. Where else flourished as colorful a journalist of the ferries and their commuters as San Francisco's Earl Ennis during the trans-Bay heyday? What other building so typifies an era of transportation to this very day so much as the Ferry Building at the foot of Market Street? And say — has anyone seen Peg-Leg Pete, the one-legged seagull lately? He, like John the Chinaman, beloved vendor of nickel bags of peanuts for time out of mind, hasn't been seen for far too long and both are presumed to be — well, rather say "out of circulation" than any other expression.

And what about "the Caruso of the ferries," that operatic-voiced young deckhand on the Southern Pacific ferries, who delighted the passengers with selections from the favorite scores while helping with the mooring lines when the boat docked? The only present information indicates that he made appearances in the vaudeville houses in San Francisco and Oakland, played a few club dates, and then retired from the public eye.

Then there was the one-armed deafened mute who carried a large supply of lavender packed in envelopes. The front of each of these explained that this was the man's only means of a livelihood. When the boat had gotten under way, he would go into the top deck saloon, drop an envelope into each person's lap in rapid succession, then double back after the travelers had had a chance to read the message and either pick up the sale price of the packet or the packet itself if it was a case of "no sale." Then he would repeat the performance on the other side of the saloon, and finally both sides of the main deck.

When the Key System placed the *Peralta* and the *Yerba Buena* in service, both sported small mahogany stands containing the telephone directories of San Francisco and Oakland for ready reference by travelers so that they could prepare phone calls while en route. For many weeks after the boats began to carry the crowds of commuters from "San Francisco's bedroom," one could always get a "bite" from the intended victim by walking through the lower deck where the "fall guy" would be seated and call out in bellboy fashion, "Telephone call for Mr. Blank on the top deck!" Particularly effective if Mr. Blank had been reading his morning newspaper, he generally could be counted on to at least enter the topdeck saloon before realizing the hoax that had been perpetrated and retiring in confusion amidst the guffaws and laughter of the group who had been quietly tipped off in advance.

Christmas was always a happy season on the ferries. A volunteer committee on arrangements would get together and trim a Christmas tree for exhibition the morning before Christmas Eve. The companies themselves generally had a token gift to present to the travelers on the morning boats, these taking the form of commutation book covers or token-holders. Santa Claus would invariably appear during the voyage to kiss giggly short-skirted stenographers for the benefit of the press photographers who were always on hand to record these happy trips.

His twice-a-day ferry jaunt was generally one of complete relaxation and enjoyment for the average commuter. In the morning, he read his paper while ensconced in his favorite seat, located in that particular part of the boat which for him held a certain appeal. Had he been a later riser and missed his breakfast at home, he could always "go downstairs" and take his morning repast in the restaurant which was operated for his convenience. There he would rub elbows with fellow late-rising commuters, occasionally spilling his coffee into his saucer when some absent-minded individual pushed his elbows out an inch too far in turning the pages of his paper. The trip on all the ferry lines was of sufficient duration between Oakland, Alameda, Richmond, Sausalito, and San Francisco to permit the consumption of a substantial meal with no loss of time. The service, by and large, was fast and courteous and the quality of the food exceptionally high, considering the handicap of space in which it was prepared.

On all the ferryboats save the Key System's the restaurants were operated by commissary departments of the respective companies. On the Key System, however, the eating facilities were maintained by the National Service Company after March 9, 1925; previous to that they were also operated directly by the Key System through the Key System Service Company. Key chefs were as well trained in the culinary art as the chefs on other lines but they were especially noted for three dishes in particular: "Key Route Corned Beef Hash," a particularly succulent rendition of this all-time favorite dish; "Key Route Apple Pie," made doubly good with a scoop of vanilla ice cream; and "Key Route Coffee," apparently a blend especially packed for the Key System since it was a flavor that couldn't be matched elsewhere.

The Southern Pacific, in addition to the restaurant facilities, also operated a buffet counter on the lower deck, featuring standup service of coffee and doughnuts in the morning, sandwiches and milk at noon, and hot-dogs and various beverages in the early evening.

The men who manned the ferryboats were of a class which has all but vanished from the sight of the watchful eye of the Ferry Building tower. Their achievements and their records are all but legends of a distant past. But it was not always so, for the ferry captain and his faithful crew were a part of San Francisco, a basic necessity to its growth and progress.

The lot of the ferry navigator, captain, or mate, whoever he might be, was not a particularly enviable one. Sometimes, of course, the assignment was an easy one and in calm spring and autumn days the ferryboat plied her whitewaked course beneath clear sunstreamed skies on a Bay of lake-like blue. The delightful clearness of the city so refreshingly washed by a spring shower or a fresh sea breeze rendered every vista from the pilot house a scene of loveliness meant for lasting duration. The bow lookout gazed back at the wheelhouse with his approving nod as the captain held his course, for the lookout's task was all but superfluous in the warm clear air. But when the thick fog obscured the navigator's vision, the lookout was a most necessary member of the navigating team.

No particular season can be designated as the "fog season" in San Francisco. In bygone years, the fogs have been thicker in November, but, oddly enough, it seems that since the ferryboats have left San Francisco Bay the fogs have been lighter than before. This, at least, is the opinion of retired ferry captains who no longer have to contend with this problem. Notwithstanding the dense fog, hundreds upon hundreds of safe crossings have been made in close to the usual running time without mishaps and the crowds of passengers have been safely delivered to their destinations without inconvenience.

The record of the ferries remains an enviable one — a record of which they may well be proud, for in the height of Bay travel, over fifty ferries plied the various routes simultaneously, each carefully missing one another, the river steamers, and all the inbound and outbound ocean traffic. The few collisions which occurred will be detailed in later chapters, but many near-collisions were fortunately avoided by skillful navigation, the ferries being a noteworthily mode of travel.

In foggy weather, it was customary for the captain to order the first officer to handle the wheel while the former directed all his energies to listening for recognized and established bells and horns and the signals of passing ships. A lookout was posted on the bow of the vessel within sight of the pilot house, and it was his duty to point in the direction of the last audible fog whistle from an established installation or of the blast from another boat. The directional point was noted by the captain who confirmed his own opinion of the sound most recently detected. The ferry's own whistle was blown with monotonous regularity for the benefit of nearby ships.

It is interesting to note that there were no navigational aids of a mechanical nature at the command of the ferry captain. He had no radar, no loran, no radio direction finder, gyroscopic compass, fathometer, or any of the accepted devices which now are deemed so indispensable to the modern mariner. He had only a standard compass at his disposal — which he seldom consulted. Navigation was accomplished almost entirely by sight and ear, for the ferry captain was almost always too perilously close to land to be able to make use of these instrumental aids to the seafaring sailor. Captain John Leale of the Southern Pacific Company, formerly a river pilot, referred to the ferryman as a "tule sailor." The story is told of a river pilot who changed his course in a particular place during inclement weather only when he heard the bark of a dog known to inhabit the shore at this particular spot. One foggy day, the pilot was steering his craft up the river, reached the turning point — but unbeknown to him, the dog had died! The result: One boat on the beach! It was often that close in Bay and river navigation.

The departures and landings of the ferryboats were carried on with a minimum of flurry and fanfare, occurring so frequently that the crews became highly adept and proficient with their duties at the commencement and termination of each ferry trip. The double-end ferryboat was designed to make a quick and easy landing, the ferry slips and wharves being designed to permit the docking of a vessel in as short a time as possible.

By carefully estimating his tide and cross currents, the ferry skipper was able to adjust his speed to suit and ultimately to glide straight into his allotted gaping, pile-studded slip. As soon as the vessel nosed into the mouth of the slip so that rudder control was no longer required, a deckhand stepped to the bow and removed the keeper pin from the forward

Pulling the rudder pin was an unending task on the Bay ferryboat; it marked the climax of a delightful trip.

rudder, thus unlocking it for the following trip in the opposite direction. After tieing up, the keeper pin was placed in the after rudder as it would become the forward rudder on the next voyage. Steering was accomplished entirely by the after rudder on all vessels except the *Peralta* and the *Yerba Buena* where both rudders were used synchronously to turn the ship.

As the vessel approached the apex of the slip, a deckhand stood prepared on either side with bowlines in hand, ready to toss the loop around the giant iron hooks attached to the innermost piling. These hooks were placed intermittently at various levels to accommodate the vessel at various heights of tide. Once the loop end was securely hooked, another deckhand would pull the bowline tight and make fast to a huge cast cleat on the deck. This entire operation took place in full view of the passengers awaiting to debark and it will be long remembered by all who rode the ferries. The next step was the lowering of the gangplank from an apron which was hydraulically adjusted throughout the day to suit tidal conditions. The gangplank was one-man-operated as it was sensitively counterbalanced to a man's weight. As soon as the gangplank was dropped, the forechain was cast aside, the light rope which had kept the waiting passengers back during the foregoing forecastle operations was released, the crowd surged forward to walk up the ramp, through the Ferry Building exits, and on out front to board the streetcars which turned on a loop at the foot of Market Street. The entire tieing-up operation took only a minute or two, but to the passengers impatiently awaiting the end of the journey and their business beyond the Ferry Building, it seemed much longer.

Tieing up to dolphins or in places other than a ferry slip, the job was different. Without the V-shaped slip to guide the craft, lines had to be passed ashore and made fast when slack, while a deck crew warped the vessel to her moorings with the hand capstan. This affair was an interesting unit, a holdover from sailing ships and other small ocean-going craft which had no powered deck machinery. At the top of the capstan was the driving hub wherein poles could be inserted. The deckhands then walked 'round and 'round the capstan hub while the friction dogs on the lower trackway clanked noisily into place to assure no reversal of the gypsy head.

Another relic of the sailing ship era was the ferryboat's anchor, an old-fashioned anchor with a folding stock. It was usually stowed on bow or stern, a massive casting in full view, to be looked upon with awe by most small boys and many grownups as well. It was always a mystery to the passengers as to how this anchor was ever weighed or handled at all. There were few occasions for its use, but it was always impressive. It looked exactly like what an anchor should look like and it had nothing about it which in any way resembled the unromantic stockless self-homing anchors of modern ocean-going ships. It was the anchor which was reproduced as the symbol of the mariner and, above all, it lent a decided nautical touch to the otherwise unseaworthy appearing craft to which it was assigned.

A ferry sailing was conducted with such perfect timing as to be hardly noticed by the passengers. As soon as the passenger gate was closed at the

The old hand capstan, born of sailing ship days, still serves the ferryboat's simple wants in deck machinery.

ROY GRAVES PHOTO

Ferry Building, the deckhands cast off the bow lines in a matter of seconds. The second mate supervised the rapid raising of the gangplank by the shore crew, then waved a hand to the first officer in the pilot house, which was the signal to proceed. The double-end ferries had two pilot houses, one at each end of the hurricane deck. The pilot house visible to the second mate at the time he cast off was the after one, but since the vessel was always under the control of the forward pilot house, the order to sail had to be relayed there by bell cord. This cord passed through the engine room and when it was pulled it could be heard by the engineer. This always alerted him that it was time to leave the dock so he always had time to jump to his throttle. The captain in the forward pilot house sounded the huge brass whistle on the side of the smokestack, the paddle wheels slowly began to turn, and the vessel glided out of the slip.

The last step in setting sail was to remove the rudder keeper pin if that chore had been forgotten or had the pin been stubborn on the incoming trip. As long as the rudder remained locked, the pilot had no control of his craft. However, on leaving the slip the steering engine could be operated from the forward pilot house, thus moving the rudder slightly and in that manner the keeper pin was usually freed sufficiently to be removed. Once out, it meant "full speed ahead." On night sailings, an additional task to be performed was the closing of the blinds on all forward windows so that the light from the cabin would not reflect on the foredeck and impair navigation from a totally dark wheelhouse.

The earlier ferries were all of wood construction, and the joiner work to be found in the cabin interiors was the product of painstaking workmanship of highly skilled craftsmen. The panels were of the finest hardwoods, with carved trim of intricate design, accentuated by various elaborate moldings at the panel's edge. This type of interior decoration was to be found only in the older ferryboats, for the newer craft displayed none of the fine wood artwork to be found on passenger ferries built in the years prior to 1900. For the most part, the paneling was of the darker woods which were the vogue of the Victorian era, and the appointments were in keeping with the formal scheme of things. Red plush adorned the seats in the cabin of the finer boats, and the glass lamp shades were splendid examples of the chandelier maker's art.

Ornately turned wooded stanchions of slender proportion dotted the cabin's interior, gracefuly supporting the stringers and deck beams of the deck overhead. Carvings and design were often carried even to these fittings, and drawing-room comfort and atmosphere was extended to the passenger on his ferry travels.

On the *Tamalpais* and the *San Pablo* the ventilating windows on the raised dome center section of the hurricane deck were constructed of ornately etched glass bearing illustrations of famous ships and ferries. These windows were most interesting to observe, and formed a mural which, when illuminated by golden sunlight, was a great attraction on these particular boats.

ROBERT PARKINSON PHOTO

Fine joinerwork marked the cabin interiors of the ferryboat's upper deck. **This** expansive view of the interior of the *Piedmont's* cabin shows the woodworker's carvings and other appointments of an ornate interior.

Another glass feature of many of the finer passenger boats was the set of glass windows located in the bulkhead between the engine fidley and the main cabin. Here the passengers could view the main engine in motion while the vessel was under way, or at least the main connecting rod between the walking beam and the main crank. It was always the fervent hope of all youngsters making the ferry trip that their accompanying adult would take seats close to the fidley windows so that small noses could continually be pressed against the window pane that separated them from the magic connecting rod whose up-and-down motion held them so utterly spellbound. A wise mother always did well to consent to sit in such a location, for it meant that not a peep would be heard from the enraptured offspring so long as the glistening rod kept up its fascinating motion. And many a grown child, too, stood watching at the wondrous window where the hypnotic engine worked with irresistable enchantment.

The great art of engine gazing through the windows of the cabin deck came to an abrupt ending one day in 1922 when the steamer *Sausalito* was making the run from San Francisco to Sausalito. The walking beam broke in a critical spot, and the main connecting rod tore loose, taking with it a good portion of the center of the hurricane deck. At the same time, the walking beam clattered down into the cabin in fragmentary condition, creating a panic among the passengers. Shortly thereafter, all of the windows which afforded a view of the engine were boarded up, hiding in ostrich-like fashion the peril that existed behind them. Much of the fascination of the ferryboat was removed when the fidley windows were covered and the ferry rider lost one of the most pleasurable pastimes afforded by the colorful trip.

Most of the double-end passenger ferries had two decks for passengers, the lower or main deck, and the upper or cabin deck. Seats were arranged in a permanent fashion, being for the most part benches with backs in varying degrees of elegance and ornate decoration. No attempt was made to enhance the appearance of the seats on the lower deck in particular, the cabin deck seats being bedecked in lavish finery. Usually there was a restaurant on an orlop deck below the main deck in a location not otherwise taken up by machinery, fuel, or water tanks and storerooms. The uppermost deck, which was clear except for the pilot houses, was referred to as the hurricane deck.

To all who knew the ferries, the long lines of express and baggage carts which clattered their rollicking way on and off the boats at either end of the journey will always be a vivid recollection. Since most of the passenger ferries, the Southern Pacific, Northwestern Pacific, Western Pacific, Santa

Fire and boat drill always livened a trip across the Bay. Here the deckhands of a Southern Pacific steamer make ready to put a boat in the water.

Fe, and also the Key Route during the operation of the Sacramento Northern trains on its pier, were incidental to the operation of a main-line railroad business, mail and baggage could easily be transferred from the railroad baggage cars onto these small carts for distribution at the San Francisco terminus. In like manner, the carts were loaded at the Ferry Building, run onto the boat, then towed by small, noisy, gas-propelled runabouts to the waiting baggage or mail car of an outgoing train. The carts were high-wheeled, top-heavy, flimsy-looking vehicles, with no refinements of design, unpossessed of any riding qualities and somewhat unmanageable, but still a boisterous part of ferry operation. In the early days, these four-wheeled vans were dignifiedly trundled on and off the boat behind a reliable draft horse who took his job seriously and never once gave a thought to frivolities. But, as the motor age encroached, the gasoline jitney superseded the horse and added speed to the caravans of carts, much to the latter's suffering. The clatter, bang and din was stepped up in an ever-increasing tempo that indicated a departure from the Victorian era, even in so lowly a field as the baggage-shuttling business. The one exception to this mad snap-the-whip of carts was the movement of a deceased's remains; the standard-appearing, four-handled redwood shipping case was always handled individually aboard the boat by a quartet of deckhands who always gently rolled their pious cargo aboard, placed it apart from the strings of other carts and, after carefully blocking the wheels to prevent any untoward movement, doffed their hats reverently and then went about their other duties.

The horses that pulled the carts in the early days were often quartered on the boat. It was even no rarity before the turn of the century to see stockmen herd their cattle to town, driving them onto the ferryboat into a roped-off pen provided for the purpose. Many of these trips were made without incident, some with alarming circumstances growing out of the hauling of the barnyard passengers. In the early Twenties, a cattleman brought his stock to town on the steamer *Eureka* from Sausalito. The event was to be one of the last of its kind and the crew was somewhat rusty in the correct procedure of attending to the bovine bureaucrats. The rope pen was inadequate, the occupants boisterous and somewhat inquisitive. It didn't take them long to effect an escape from their hempen pen in the course of the journey and to begin a merry round of hobnobbing with the two-legged passengers. One thing led to another, and soon the cattle were trying the stairs, demanding — and getting — attention in the restaurant, and herding a flock of frightened passengers hither and yon in wild disorder. The affray actually lasted but a comparatively few minutes until peace was restored and a series of stout ropes were pressed into service to restrain the boisterous bovines, but while it lasted, the incident afforded a few exciting moments in the course of the journey.

Almost every ferry passenger was intrigued by the seagull throngs which accompanied the vessel from terminal to terminal. A good portion of the dry-food purchased at the restaurants aboard the boats was not bought for human consumption but was thrown in small bits by fascinated passengers

SPERRY GYROSCOPE COMPANY PHOTO

Wheelhouse of the modern diesel-electric ferryboat *Stockton* showing pilot house
controls

to the aerial soloists which escorted the ship. Sailing, soaring, gliding, fighting over scraps in a series of quick dives, the seagull was a constant source
of entertainment. His raucous cries, his graceful flights, his greedy nature,
all were an intimate part of ferry travel. Earl Ennis, in his "Ferry Tales,"
even conjectured at some length upon the then contemplated abandonment
of the ferries, and, thereupon, of the future fate of the seagull who had
bummed his meals from ferry riders for nearly a century. There is no evi-
dence of mass starvation having taken place upon the discontinuance of
ferry travel on the Bay, but the seagull certainly had to make some rapid
economic adjustments when the walking beams stopped rocking and the
paddle wheels churned no more.

As a segment of the public continues to bewail the fact that people continually jump off the bridges of San Francisco Bay, the morbid but academic question is naturally raised as to where the accomplished suicides
with a nautical setting took place before the bridges were built. The answer
is, of course, off the ferryboats. Although jumping off the deck of a ferry
could not be called an advisable way of committing suicide, many people
tried it. The height of the cabin deck, or even the hurricane deck for that

matter, was not sufficiently above the waterline to kill a person by impact and drowning is a method of self-destruction not easily accomplished. If the paddle wheel or the propeller did not crush the would-be suicide, his chances of survival were almost one hundred per cent in his favor. Passengers have jumped off the bow of a moving ferryboat, to be picked up a few minutes later just astern of the vessel, wet but uninjured. The record for *curiosa* in this respect probably belongs to Captain August Palmer of the steamer *Cazadero* when a passenger leaped into the water on the inbound voyage to the Ferry Building at 11:15 o'clock one cold January night. The *Cazadero* had a layup of an hour and a half at the Ferry Building before returning to Sausalito. The passenger was not missed when he jumped and his method of suicide might never have been discovered had he not survived. Leaving promptly at 12:45 a.m. from the Ferry Building, Captain Palmer saw a dark object in the water, flashed his searchlight on it, and discovered his former passenger, chilled but unharmed. He was promptly fished out of the water and told his amazing story of floating in the Bay for better than an hour and a half to the captain. Crew members instantly recognized him when they brought him aboard. He said the cold had decidedly changed his mind on the subject of drowning.

One of the traditions of San Francisco Bay was the decoration of the ferryboats on holidays and other gala occasions. Besides carrying banners of every color of the rainbow, all the old-time boats were equipped with a house flag, a vessel flag, and a commission pennant. And it seemed that the smaller the boat, the longer the commission pennant. Standard practice was to have four ensign staffs, two at each end of the vessel, to fly the American flag. Free-lance decoration was often the most colorful, although not always adhering to maritime law. In later years, the vessels carried but two flag staffs, one for the ensign and one for the jack. On special outings, bunting was festooned around the upper deck, and at Christmas time garlands of greens were draped on railings and house fronts. Each vessel had a tree on the masthead and one in the cabin. Vessel decoration only served to reflect the pride the crews had in their boats. Competition between the vessels was often keen and, although no prizes were offered and nothing was at stake, the ferryman thought well of his boat and his work. Accordingly, he took every opportunity he had to display his ship in the best possible light.

The ferry engineer kept a well polished engine room to be continually on display to the full view of his passengers. He was proud of his engines and the crew that ran them. In one respect, the engineer had a marvelous opportunity to display his tastes in that audible and ornamental decoration, the steam whistle. On each boat there were two whistles, one operated from each pilot house. The whistles were usually the design of the original engineer of the vessel, and some of the mellow tones produced were original, distinctive, and of such outstanding quality as to identify the ferryboat whenever and wherever the blast was blown. Most ferrymen were able to name any vessel simply by hearing its whistle, a most valuable aid when fog

SOUTHERN PACIFIC PHOTO

The ferry clock tower, trademark of San Francisco's waterfront, stands sentry as the *Hayward* (left) sets out for the Key Route Oakland wharf, the *Santa Clara* leaves for the Oakland Mole, and the *Sierra Nevada* leaves for Alameda in the heyday of the ferries. The Bay Bridge, soon to spell the ferries' doom, appears in the background.

closed in on the Bay. By hearing the familiar sounds in their accustomed directions, the ferry pilot knew his course was true.

The ferryman and the ferryboat served San Francisco, Metropolitan Oakland, and the other communities of the East Shore in an immeasurable way. They traveled millions of miles together and never left the harbor in their voyages, but those miles were the miles that built the cities around San Francisco Bay. No chronicle of anything pertaining to San Francisco Bay, therefore, would ever be complete without "A Salute to the Ferryboat!"

CHAPTER II

THE RIVERBOAT
CONQUERS THE BAY

 SLEEPY MEXICAN PROVINCE of Alta California, undisturbed and unexplored, lay easy prey to the horde of goldseekers which flocked to the state in the Days of '49. Missing from the new frontier were most of the comforts of home for, in primitive California, the advance of civilization had suffered a severe setback. Men went to the unexplored gold fields on foot and on muleback, bought their supplies at exorbitant prices — when supplies were even available — and had to make the best of it.

The scene of most of the activity and outfitting center for the gold-field caravans was Sacramento, just one hundred and twenty miles by river from the seaport of San Francisco. It became imperative that a transportation service be established between San Francisco and Sacramento and the cry was heard for boats and more boats, suitable or unsuitable, to handle the Sacramento River traffic in passengers and freight. There were neither boatmen nor boatbuilders in California, and the home product, when it finally appeared, was decidedly overshadowed by the imported model.

Incredible as it may seem, the early river steamers made the journey from the Atlantic seaboard to California 'round the Horn, attempting journeys in the flimsy unseaworthy ships that would make the voyages of Columbus seem no more risky than a passage on the *Queen Mary*. Perhaps the most daring of them all was the trip of Captain Ned Wakeman aboard the steamer *New World,* a noble vessel launched in New York and immediately attached for liens upon the completion of her construction. But the undaunted Wakeman finally shook himself loose from the sheriff's deputies and, unprepared as he was, put out to sea one stormy night in 1849. One hundred and fifty days later, this poor man's Magellan sailed into San Francisco harbor on January 19, 1850, with a pay load of passengers picked up in Central and South American ports, for the goldseekers would ride anything, at any price, if the destination was California! The circumstances of Wakeman's sailing were unique, his passage heroic, but it was duplicated many times as the need for river boats increased in California.

Old timers, such as the *Amelia, Antelope,* and the *Yosemite,* together with contemporaries, pioneered the Sacramento River for their owners, the California Steam Navigation Company. But the pride of the fleet was the *Chrysopolis,* built in California in 1860 by John G. North, built as well as

The fabulous ferry of the Fifties was Captain Ned Wakeman's *New World* which made the voyage 'round the horn to San Francisco from the Atlantic seaboard in 150 days.

a river vessel was ever constructed. Carrying the now lowly-rated steam pressure of fifty pounds, the *Chrysopolis* typified the walking beam and paddle-wheeled vessel of the river era. Better than two hundred feet in length, 1,000 tons measurement, and of very shallow draft, the vessel set a record for the Sacramento - San Francisco run of five hours and nineteen minutes at an average speed of approximately twenty knots! But the keen competition and breakneck speeds of river service soon bowed to the railroad which, at first, depended on the boats for connecting service between San Francisco and Sacramento.

On September 6, 1869, the transcontinental Central Pacific Railroad opened its route from Sacramento through the San Joaquin Valley and Niles Canyon to Alameda, and passengers no longer had to transfer to the boats in Sacramento. Now they were able to ride through to Alameda and secure passage via ferryboat to the Davis Street wharf in San Francisco. This arrangement lasted but two months when the Central Pacific inaugurated service from the Oakland wharf.

Although the boats of the Central Pacific and its successor, the Southern Pacific, eventually controlled the Oakland - San Francisco ferry lanes, such was not always the case. Back in 1850, before California had yet become a state, Captain Thomas Gray placed his diminutive screw-propeller steamer *Kangaroo* on a twice-weekly schedule, both sailings subject, however, to the whims of tide and weather. The small vessel departed from the San Francisco waterfront and made a landing on the embarcadero of San Antonio Creek, now better known as the Oakland Estuary. The purpose of the ferry service was to offer excursionists a trip "across the Bay" and to permit metropolitan inhabitants an "opportunity to visit the wondrously wooded region of Contra Costa."

The *Kangaroo* was the first regularly scheduled Oakland ferryboat, although independent excursion craft had of course visited the eastern shore in earlier days. Typical fares on the *Kangaroo* were $1.00 per person, $3.00 per wagon, $3.00 per horse, and comparable fares for combinations of these classifications.

After the *Kangaroo* had made the start, business soon was on the upswing for, in 1851, a Captain Rhodes brought a small steamer around Cape Horn from New York and began regular trips between San Francisco and one of the landings in Oakland. Then following the leadership of the pioneering smaller craft, Charles Minturn, one of the more successful operators of river craft, took the former river boat *Erastus Corning,* which had appeared on the transportation scene in December, 1851, and placed her on the run between San Francisco and San Antonio Creek. Gradually the larger paddle steamers began to appear on the Oakland run, not all operating on a regular schedule, but nevertheless maintaining continual operation to the eastern shore of San Francisco Bay. Many of these vessels were in the nature of small ocean-going ships which found the ferry trade more lucrative and much easier of navigation than the hazardous trip around Cape Horn to the eastern seaboard.

Among the newcomers was the *Boston* which climaxed her brief career by being destroyed by fire, and the *Red Jacket,* which had been built as the *Empire* and later rechristened the *Kate Hayes.* The captain of the *Red Jacket* was John R. Fouratt, an ancestor of the many Captains Fouratt who served the Southern Pacific Company through numerous years of ferry operation.

Another boat to desert the rivers and sloughs for the Bay ferry trade was the *Caleb Cope,* soon followed by the *Jenny Lind.* The latter vessel enjoyed but a short life on the ferry lanes for, in April of 1853, she became the victim of a boiler explosion in the South Bay while making the run between San Francisco and Alviso, wiping herself and thirty-one unfortunate victims off the face of the earth.

The *Kangaroo* was succeeded in 1853 by a very small sidewheel steamer christened the *Hector.* This vessel was most unusual in that it was one of the few paddle vessels using a system of mechanical reduction gears in the transmittal of power from the main engine to the wheel shaft.

In 1851, Oakland had been formally established as a town. With a commendable display of civic pride and with more important economic reasons to back up their actions, the city fathers gave serious consideration to the creation of a public ferry to San Francisco. Their concern in the ferry situation was not without cause, for the independent operators had been none too reliable, incapable at times of coping with the natural physical hazards of the "Creek Route" up the Estuary, and continually carrying on private rate wars between themselves which frequently all but eliminated the ferry. In 1852, Charles Minturn gained considerable backing from the steamboat men and organized the Contra Costa Steam Navigation Company. His associates, like himself, were reliable men with reputations for conducting large scale business in a manner beneficial to both the public and the operator alike so the town looked to the Minturn company to operate the public ferry.

Since the Contra Costa Steam Navigation Company was already equipped with suitable vessels and was the possessor of adequate terminal space, a new ordinance was passed by the Oakland trustees in March of 1853, creating the public ferry authority. At the same time, the trustees entered into a contract with E. R. Carpentier, one of Minturn's associates, to operate the ferry for a twenty-year period in consideration of a certain percentage of the net profits which were to be paid by the navigation company to the town.

The Contra Costa Steam Navigation Company immediately placed the *Erastus Corning* and the *Kate Hayes* in the new service. But these vessels were soon returned to the river service from whence they came, for, on December 26, 1853, the Minturn company placed in service the new steamer *Clinton*, under the command of Captain L. B. Edwards. The *Clinton* made three trips daily, to be joined on September 15, 1857, by the *Contra Costa*, built at the San Francisco shipyard of John G. North, thus increasing the service to three daily round trips. The boats departed from the Davis Street wharf in San Francisco at 9:30 a.m., 1:30 p.m., and 5:00 p.m. From Oakland, the boats whistled out of the pier at the foot of Broadway on San Antonio Creek at 7:30 a.m., 12 noon, and 3:30 p.m.

The original fares were decidedly high, commutation rates being as high as $20.00 per month. However, public pressure and increased passenger traffic served to secure the reduction of the "commuter" fare to $10.00 per month on September 28, 1857. Moreover, in the early part of 1858, the Minturn line hit another snag in rate-making when a rival company inaugurated competitive operation from Oakland to San Francisco. This was the San Antonio Steam Navigation Company, under the presidency of James B. LaRue, operating the steamer *San Antonio*, with Captain John Fouratt as master. The initial commutation fare of the new company was $5.00 and Minturn immediately cut his rate to match, and even went lower on single-ride fares.

While the bitter rivalry ensued, Minturn resorted to the courts and attempted to obtain an injunction against the rival company on the grounds that his rights, which were granted him by the trustees of Oakland, were being infringed upon. But the courts failed to grant his injunction on the ground that the trustees could not grant Minturn the exclusive right to operate a ferry because they possessed no such right to give. So Minturn was forced to live in competition with his rival who, in August of 1858, started construction of a new ferryboat to be christened the *Oakland*.

The Contra Costa Steam Navigation Company with its *Clinton* and *Contra Costa,* and the San Antonio Steam Navigation Company with the *San Antonio* and the *Oakland,* settled down in 1858 to a grim battle of survival. Fares were stabilized by mutual agreement of the competing parties, but each tried to undermine the welfare of the other in every way possible, particularly in the field of Bay navigation itself. The Oakland Estuary was a narrow strip of water in the Fifties, and the churning paddle steamers ran neck and neck down the restricted channel, vieing for position. Each would try to run the other onto the shallow sandbar at the mouth of the creek and it has been stated that the pilots even kept rifles handy to insure "co-operation" from the rival skippers.

Fate dealt Minturn another hard blow in April, 1859, when the boilers of the *Contra Costa* exploded; thus, the steamers of the San Antonio company outnumbered him two to one while the *Contra Costa* was undergoing repairs. On the other hand, the sandbar at the mouth of San Antonio Creek which had so hampered navigation in the past, was now dredged out and the channel widened to two hundred feet, which was entirely to the satisfaction of the rival companies. But competition had been too keen for both operators, and in August of 1859 they drew up an agreement to operate their boats jointly_ splitting the traffic between them while retaining their separate corporate identities.

While merrily quarreling between themselves, Minturn and LaRue exhausted their energies and resources, expending everything for what they regarded as the all-important control of the Oakland ferry traffic. But they had overlooked one important point — and that one actually spelled out the control in the cases of all the passenger ferries: Neither company offered transportation in conjuction with the ferry which would transport and distribute the passengers to and from the widely-scattered settled areas of the East Bay region. When an operator would eventually appear on the scene with a feeder railway, he needed only to commence his own ferryboat operations in conjunction with the rail line — and Minturn and LaRue would be licked.

Such an operator did turn up in the form of the San Francisco & Oakland Railroad Company which commenced operation on the second of September, 1863, and so advantageous was their position because of their local railroad operations in connection with the ferry line that Minturn had already rented his steamer *Contra Costa* to the newcomer on a basis of six round trips per day. The *Contra Costa* remained on this run for a year, at which time the Oakland railroad placed its own steamer *Louise* in service. Minturn's itinerant ferryboat was then rented to the San Francisco & Alameda Railroad Company which had been built on the shore of the island city in 1864 and which was opened to traffic on August 25 of that same year. But the Alameda company also constructed its own steamer, the *Alameda,* in 1866 — and Minturn was out in the cold again.

Relinquishing his rights to the East Bay traffic he had so energetically pioneered, Minturn looked to the North Bay where he had been operating

SOUTHERN PACIFIC PHOTO

The San Francisco & Alameda Railroad Company built the *Alameda* in 1866 to continue their ferry service to the island city which was commenced in 1864.

boats to Petaluma Creek as early as 1862, adding the *Clinton* to this route in 1863 and eventually assigning the *Contra Costa* to this service in 1866. The two veterans were eventually sold to the San Rafael & San Quentin Railroad, and the pioneer Minturn retired from the ferry transportation scene.

The Central Pacific Railroad Company had been incorporated in 1861 for the purpose of building a railroad from California to a then undetermined connection with the nearest eastern line. Promoters of the railroad were Leland Stanford, Collis P. Huntington, Charles Crocker, and Mark Hopkins. At the time they organized the railroad company, these four were merchants in Sacramento, but they proved to be an unbeatable team in the financing and construction of a railroad deemed by many at the time to be a physical impossibility. Following the organization, eight hard construction years brought final completion and connection with the Union Pacific on May 10, 1869, near Promontory Point, Utah. Most of the crucial material for the line had to be shipped from the Atlantic seaboard to San Francisco, then transshipped to Sacramento via river steamer. At the time, the "Big Four" were much too concerned with railroad building to venture into the realm of steamboat business.

But, since it was then impractical to continue the railroad into the City of San Francisco regardless of route, it became apparent that only in conjunction with ferry service could the Central Pacific properly function. So,

in 1867-8, Stanford, Huntington, Hopkins, and Crocker gradually purchased the controlling stock of both the San Francisco & Oakland Railroad
Company and the San Francisco & Alameda Railroad Company. The facilities of both companies were made available to the transcontinental railroad
and both were eventually used by it.

When the first Overland Route train rolled into Alameda over the Niles
Canyon trackage, it was the former San Francisco & Alameda Railroad Company steamer *Alameda* which connected with the train and brought the passengers across the Bay to San Francisco on September 6, 1869. This use of
the Alameda wharf was temporary since the Central Pacific was engaged
in making extensive alterations and repairs to the Oakland wharf to accommodate the anticipated increase in traffic it would be subjected to because
of the additional burden of overland freight and passengers. This work
was completed by November 8, 1869, and on that day the overland trains
commenced to operate along Seventh Street in Oakland to the Oakland
wharf.

At the time the Central Pacific gained control of the local railroad companies, the fleet of East Bay lines consisted of the first *Oakland,* the first
Alameda, the *Washoe,* and *El Capitan.* Of these vessels the *Oakland* was
the smallest and the oldest, being a sidewheeler of 285 gross tons. Next was
the *Washoe,* a converted sidewheeler from the Sacramento River, built in
1864, measuring 580 gross tons, and placed in service between the Oakland
wharf and San Francisco in 1865. The *Alameda,* built in 1866, was 193 feet
in length and was a double-end, sidewheel steamer. Newest, largest, and
pride of the fleet was *El Capitan,* built in 1868, under the direction of the
Central Pacific. The vessel was 194 feet in length, was registered at 982
gross tons, and was a double-end sidewheel steamer.

The Central Pacific hauled a good quantity of freight into Oakland's
wharf and this freight had to be transferred to floating equipment in order
to be received in San Francisco. Loading from freight car onto the boat
and unloading the boat at the opposite end of the journey caused a double
handling which did not exactly lend itself to the reduction of freight rates.
Consequently, the railroad company had built for their account a freight-
car transfer steamer, named the *Thoroughfare,* to run from Oakland to the
railroad's Second Street Wharf in San Francisco. An isolated yard in San
Francisco permitted classification and routing of cars to firms to which
they had been consigned. The transfer of freight cars by ferryboat and
barge has been an activity on San Francisco Bay which is not likely to be
discontinued unless or until a San Francisco Bay Bridge with rail trackage
be built.

About the time that the *Thoroughfare* was ready for service, the Oakland
Long Wharf was completed. This wharf was built from the mainland over
the shoal water between deep water and the shore. Dock facilities at the
end of the wharf permitted ocean steamers and sailing ships to berth on
the Oakland side of the Bay, and a single track was provided for railroad
cars the full length of this two-mile structure. The freight transfer slips

ROBERT McFARLAND PHOTO

Her flags flying from every staff, the little *El Capitan* is depicted above operating between South Vallejo and Vallejo Junction.

SOUTHERN PACIFIC PHOTO

The car float *Transit* carried the freight trains from Oakland Long Wharf to San Francisco yards in the early days of the Southern Pacific.

were established on the Oakland Long Wharf rather than the Central Pacific's Oakland wharf which was already overcrowded with both local and mainline passenger business. The *Thoroughfare* commenced the freight transfer service on January 16, 1871, while on March 6, 1876, a larger vessel, the *Transit,* was added. The *Thoroughfare* could handle sixteen freight cars of the short construction then prevalent. She was 248 feet long and her engine developed 400 horespower, which was little enough when considered alongside of the 1,500 horsepower which was average for a ferryboat at the time of cessation of service. The *Transit* was 338 feet long, 1,566 gross tons, and 1,533 horsepower.

In stating the particulars of the *Transit's* physical characteristics, it might be well to draw attention to the peculiar fact that the gross tonnage and horsepower of ships, whether they be bay ferries or ocean liners, are invariably equal or close to being equal. There is no particular reason for this to be a truth, and the designing naval architect probably never gives the matter a thought, but such is strangely often the case. The academic definition of horsepower, of course, is the standard theoretical unit of the rate of work equal to 33,000 pounds lifted one foot in one minute.

Gross tonnage is one of the most misunderstood terms in our language. Even persons in the marine field talk glibly about it without having an exact idea of what it means. Only a general definition can be given, as it is only the United States Admeasurer, who functions under the direction of the Collector of Customs, who can quote the gross tonnage of any given ship. However, the gross tonnage is the cubic capacity of the interior of the hull and superstructure, certain spaces excepted, divided by one hundred. Having thus defined the two terms, the close approximation of the two for any given vessel seems strange, indeed, but a search of the records will disclose how often these figures follow each other.

In its rapid growth, the Central Pacific kept right on absorbing smaller companies, feeder lines, and competitors alike. One of these was the California Pacific Railroad, which had built a rail line from South Vallejo to a point on the Sacramento River opposite the city of Sacramento. This competitor was not so formidable as a rail rival, but it operated more than twenty steamers up the Sacramento River. The California Pacific failed in 1871, and the Central Pacific gained control of the company and took over its trackage and river craft as of that date. This marked the beginning of the Sacramento River traffic which the railroad carried on until 1930, referring to it as the "Netherlands Route." Famous vessels of the Southern Pacific's fleet of river boats in later years included the *Navajo, Seminole, Apache, Modoc,* and *Cherokee.* The story of the river boats will have to await another writing, for it is as long as the tale of the Bay ferries and just as historic and colorful.

For many years the railroad operated ferries between Vallejo Junction and South Vallejo, this service giving the people of Vallejo an opportunity to avail themselves of the Central Pacific's rail service on the opposite side of the Bay. Again it was the riverboat which was impressed into the crossing

SOUTHERN PACIFIC PHOTO

The *Julia,* first oil burner of San Francisco Bay, blew up at South Vallejo in 1888 and discouraged oil burning on ferryboats until after the turn of the century.

SOUTHERN PACIFIC PHOTO

Up Mare Island Channel steams the *Amador* against a backdrop of the Navy Yard and the Aden Bros. sternwheel steamer *Sunol* in the right-hand foreground.

of the straits, the *Amelia,* the *Julia,* and the *Amador* being the three princi-pal boats engaged in this operation. The *Amelia* was a vessel of 386 gross tons and a sidewheeler. She was placed in service on the Vallejo Junction - South Vallejo run on December 28, 1879, and continued in the service of the Central Pacific until she was sold in 1882. The *Amelia* was succeeded by the *Julia,* a larger vessel which had been in service on the Sacramento River. The *Julia* had the distinction of being the first vessel on the Bay to burn oil in her boiler furnaces. In defense of this bold step, it should be pointed out that there had to be a pioneer who would inaugurate the use of crude oil as fuel, but this was not the proper time nor was the *Julia* the proper vessel. The equipment necessary for oil burning was not as yet successfully developed nor were the ferryboat firemen experienced in the use of the new fuel. Their eyewitness stories as to what went wrong were never obtainable because the *Julia* blew up at Vallejo on February 27, 1888, and coal burning was hurriedly resumed.

The calamity of the *Julia* brought another river veteran onto the scene to try its hand at the South Vallejo run. This vessel was the single-ended *Amador* which had been rebuilt into a double-end ferry in 1878. The *Amador* was 200 feet long and carried three hundred passengers, doing a faithful job for the railroad until her retirement in 1904. She served as a clubhouse for the University of California rowing crews after she was withdrawn from

ROY GRAVES PHOTO

From the bones of old *Chrysopolis* the Central Pacific steamer *Oakland* was built to serve a long sixty-five years on San Francisco Bay. Gushing the black cinders of her coal-burning days, she made many a crossing on the San Francisco - Oak-land route.

service. Her career ended in a blaze of glory in 1915 when she was blown up in a fireboat demonstration at the Panama-Pacific Exposition in San Francisco.

The Central Pacific Railroad terminated its Alameda ferry service in 1873 and the Alameda wharf was abandoned on September 29 of the same year. Thereafter, Alameda local trains operated out of Oakland Wharf and crossed the Estuary over the Alice Street bridge to the island city.

The year 1874 saw the purchase of the old river steamer *Chrysopolis* by the Central Pacific Railroad, which company rebuilt her from stem to stern into a double-end ferryboat. Made available for service on June 2, 1875, the vessel was lengthened to 261 feet and her gross tonnage increased to 1672 tons. She was rechristened the *Oakland* and replaced the first boat of that name which had been broken up the previous year. All in all, the second *Oakland* was in service longer than any other boat on San Francisco Bay. She was rebuilt in 1898 and again in 1920. Still her walking beam creaked away and the big crank turned the paddles. When the Bay Bridge was completed, the *Oakland* wouldn't give up, although she was retired from active service, still in excellent operating condition. But early in 1940, the veteran hull caught fire while lying on the southern Alameda shore and old *Chrysopolis* gave up at last. She had carried more generations of San Franciscans and Metropolitan Oaklanders in her glorious lengthy lifetime than any other ferry.

Rapidly increasing business required expanded terminal facilities in San Francisco for the great Central Pacific Railroad since the company had long outgrown the Davis Street Wharf. Arrangements were finally concluded with the State Harbor Commissioners to construct new facilities on East Street, now called the Embarcadero, between the foot of Market Street and Clay Street. Immediately adjacent to the wharves, the Central Pacific built a passenger station, a huge wooden frame structure with stalls on the street side for street cars. Over these stalls were painted the principal destinations which were served by the C.P.R.R., those "far-away places with strange-sounding names." Above the station shed was a small clock tower, and for over twenty years this "old Ferry Building" symbolized the "end of Market Street" of nineteenth century San Francisco. The railroad's ferryboats began landing at the old ferry building on September 4, 1875.

In 1876, the railroad made another stab at operating a ferry line up Oakland Estuary. This time a ferry slip was built at the foot of Broadway and service was inaugurated on July 1, 1876. Once again the riverboat was brought in for the newest conquest of the Bay as the Sacramento River steamer, the *Capital,* a huge vessel of approximately 2,000 gross tons, was converted into a ferry for the "Creek Route." The *Capital* was retired in 1889 and thereafter the run was shared by other vessels generally assigned to other of the railroad's ferry routes.

To give a clearer picture of the activities of the ferries after 1878, it becomes necessary at this time to describe the relocations and additions to the mainline trackage of the Central Pacific so that the reader may compre-

SOUTHERN PACIFIC PHOTO

The Central Pacific Depot at the foot of Market Street in San Francisco was a landmark of the nineteenth century. Below, the modern Ferry Building marked the consolidation of the ferry wharf facilities in one locality in 1898.

SOUTHERN PACIFIC PHOTO

The train ferry *Solano* was the largest ferryboat in the world, all 420 feet of her. Her two walking beam engines kept this behemoth rolling for 51 years on the Carquinez crossing.

The big steamer *Newark* had the largest paddle wheels of any ferryboat ever built, her 42-foot diameter wheels were exceeded in size only by the 45-foot wheels of the Pacific Mail steamer *Montana*.

hend the accompanying ferry operations. The railroad constructed a line from Oakland to Berkeley, thence to Richmond, Port Costa, and Martinez to Tracy in 1877 and 1878, thus considerably shortening the former transcontinental route via Niles Canyon. And, while skirting the south side of Carquinez Straits, the line came within a mile of the trackage inherited from the California Pacific on the opposite side of the water. If only the straits could be crossed somehow, the route to Sacramento would be lessened by many miles.

To conquer the Bay in those days, one always needed ferryboats. Now needed was a boat that could carry an entire train — including the locomotive. The answer to the problem was the giant ferry steamer *Solano*, the largest ferry of any kind in the world. Completed in 1879, the vessel was 420 feet long, registered at 3,549 gross tons, with 2,500 horsepower divided between two single-cylinder walking-beam engines, each driving one side wheel. This rather remarkable arrangement permitted easy maneuverability in the cross currents of the Straits. Service began on December 28, 1879, the vessel having been built at West Oakland within sight of the breaking up of that famous old river craft *New World*. The *New World* had pioneered the rivers and bays in the Fifties while the *Solano* carried on as the giant outgrowth of the early rivercraft in a lifetime of service that lasted more than fifty years.

In February, 1879, the *Alameda* rammed *El Capitan* while both vessels were in the service to Oakland Wharf. *El Capitan* had to be extensively reconditioned after this accident, and the *Oakland* and the *Alameda* shared the Oakland run. Extensive alterations were being accomplished on the Oakland Wharf, meanwhile, the piling and trestles being replaced by solid fills of earth and rock, and the reconstruction of the depot and trackage facilities resulted in the present Oakland Pier or "The Mole" as it has been known to native Californians. It was opened to traffic on January 22, 1882. This change enabled the railroad to operate all passenger traffic from the Oakland Pier and only freight was henceforth handled over the Oakland Long Wharf.

In 1873, the Central Pacific abandoned the wharf on the Alameda side of the Estuary, but this property did not remain inactive for long. A wave of popularity of narrow-gauge railroads had struck the West and the economies of both building and operating these miniature lines were selling points to railroad promoters. The railroad business was fascinating and very lucrative, and the solid men of prominence saw in themselves another Stanford or Huntington, Crocker, or Hopkins. From the Nevada silver mines came another "Big Four," kings of the Comstock, the Bonanza Barons of Virginia: the Messrs. Mackay, Fair, Flood, and O'Brien. James G. Fair, one-time U.S. Senator from Nevada, fascinated by the greatly expanding narrow-gauge Denver & Rio Grande, incorporated his South Pacific Coast Railroad on March 25, 1876. The projected starting place: Alameda; the projected terminal (in dreams) : the Colorado River, but the actual stopping place (because of cash on hand — or lack thereof) : Santa Cruz.

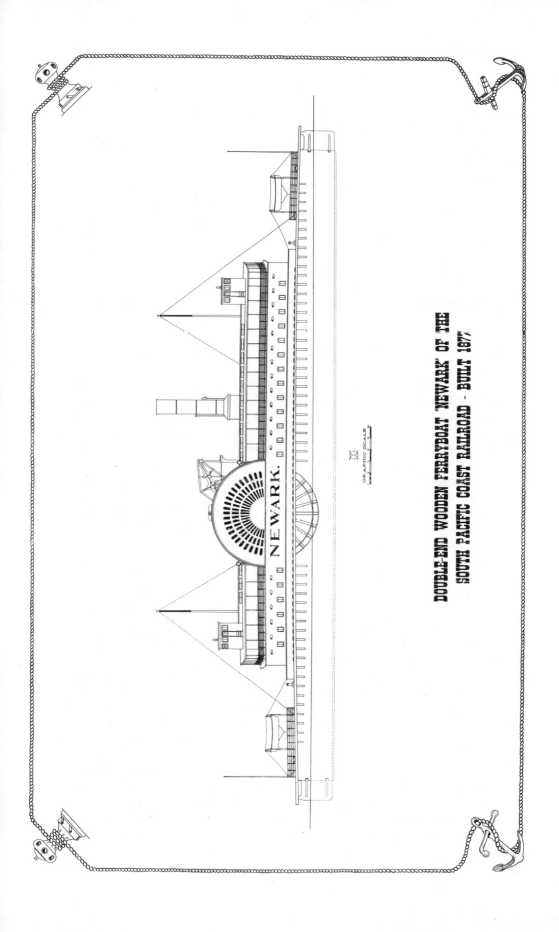

NEWARK.

GRAPHIC SCALE

DOUBLE-END WOODEN FERRYBOAT "NEWARK" OF THE
SOUTH PACIFIC COAST RAILROAD - BUILT 1877

President of the narrow-gauge South Pacific Coast was Alfred E. Davis, former mining partner of Senator Fair, who conducted most of the affairs of the railroad from his "corner" in Collins' Saloon on Montgomery Street in San Francisco. Davis was a shrewd dealer and under his direction the railroad made rapid progress.

New construction on the South Pacific Coast started in May, 1876, the point of initial construction being Dumbarton Point on the east shore of San Francisco Bay. Building materials and rails were transported to the Point by steamer, and President Davis, together with his assistant and general superintendent, Thomas Carter, often rode in the pilot house just to "watch the Cap' steer." It was on one of these private excursions that Davis struck up an acquaintance with Captain John Leale, a young and promising mariner on the Bay of San Francisco. Shortly thereafter, Davis offered Leale the post of master of the company's new ferryboat, the *Newark*. Captain Leale accepted and his name forever after became associated with that of the ferryboat as one of the foremost masters and pilots of the Bay for the South Pacific Coast Railroad.

The *Newark* was launched April 18, 1877, and completed in the latter half of that year, being ready for operation prior to the commencement of train service; thus, the new boat was used for bay excursions and the shipping of freight to Alameda prior to the opening of the railroad line. She was a tremendous boat for a mere passenger ferry, being 294 feet long, a beam of 80 feet, and a gross measurement of 1,783 tons. She had a fine big beam engine, 1,237 horsepower, and the largest paddle wheels on the Bay — 42 feet in diameter. Her wheels were exceeded in size only by one ocean-going steamer, the Pacific Mail Steamship Company's *Montana* with 45-foot wheels. Enormous brightly-painted paddle boxes were an outstanding feature of the *Newark* and they served to emphasize the girth of the wheels they covered. One of the vessel's engineers was fond of saying that the *Newark* left San Francisco and arrived in Alameda with but nine revolutions of her wheels. This was of course a gross exaggeration but it actually seemed as though but little more actual effort than that described was expended in making the crossing.

One of the remarkable differences between the *Newark* and all other ferries was the fact that her paddle shaft was on such a high center to compensate for the huge wheels that a clearance of eight feet existed between the main-deck level and the underside of the shaft. Typical of all early-day boats, the *Newark* had no steering engine and a huge double wheel in each pilot house was the means of manually controlling the rudder. On a bad tide, it took four deckhands to "hold her head" in making a difficult landing.

The South Pacific Coast Railroad was opened to traffic on March 20, 1878, the line then extending from Alameda to Newark. The ferryboat *Newark* made the inaugural trip from San Francisco to Alameda. By the first of June of the same year, the railroad had been extended to Los Gatos; also, the *Bay City*, launched May 18, 1878, had been added to the railroad's

SOUTHERN PACIFIC PHOTO

The *Bay City* leaves the South Pacific Coast (narrow gauge) wharf at Alameda Point.

fleet. The *Bay City* was 247 feet long and had a single-cylinder beam engine which developed 860 horsepower. The vessel was smaller and handier than the *Newark* and, during the first years of operation when traffic was light on the narrow-gauge line, the *Bay City* was used more frequently than the older boat.

Captain John Leale, in his *Recollections of a Tule Sailor,* related an incident which involved both the *Newark* and the *Bay City*:

"One day on my return from Alameda Point, when about five minutes out, the mainline conductor rushed up to the pilot house in a blue funk. He had come over with us a boat ahead of his passengers and had fallen asleep in the cabin and failed to go ashore. I said to him, 'Don't get excited, Tom. I'll take a chance if you will.' So on meeting the *Bay City* with Tommie's passengers aboard, I blew the whistle for her to stop; then stopped my boat and sent Tommie off to join his passengers. The first man he met going over the rail was Mr. A. E. Davis (president of the S.P.C.R.R.) who said to him, 'Where the h——l have you bin? A-fishin?' I was happy to know later that that was all the investigation held.

"Excursions and picnics were very much in vogue in those days, especially on Sundays, and some of them were tough! On the return trip, passenger cars would arrive at Alameda Point with every window broken and a scrap or two on the boat coming over would finish the day. A German picnic was safe for order. I will leave unsaid what nationality indulged in the most scrapping."

The South Pacific Coast completed its line to Santa Cruz in 1880, a special train being operated over the system from Alameda to Santa Cruz on May 23 of that year. A picnic was spread at Big Trees, just north of Santa Cruz, but tragedy struck at the gay assembly when the train jumped the track and spilled out the celebrants, killing fourteen and cancelling the entire opening day program.

During the brief independent operation of the South Pacific Coast, two more ferryboats were built for the railroad, both of them being double-enders as were their two predecessors. The steamer *Garden City* was built in 1879 and was launched on June 20 of that year. She was 243 feet long, was admeasured at 1,080 gross tons and her beam engine developed 933 horsepower. The little vessel seated but 790 passengers compared with the *Bay City's* 1,205 and the *Newark's* 1,593. The *Bay City* and the *Garden City* therefore carried on the principal business of the narrow-gauge road, the *Newark* being used at intervals when business was heavy, on excursions, or on Sundays. Last of the S.P.C. fleet was the steamer *Encinal*, launched on November 15, 1887, and completed in 1888 as a combination freight transfer and passenger ferry. This vessel was 274 feet long and carried 1,363 passengers as a capacity load.

Before the *Encinal* was completed, the South Pacific Coast Railroad was purchased by the Southern Pacific Company which had been incorporated on December 2, 1865, by Peter Donahue and associates. The Central Pacific Railroad purchased the Southern Pacific soon after its incorporation, reorganized it in 1870, and carried on much of the Central Pacific expansion in the name of the Southern Pacific. In 1884-5, the entire Central Pacific system was reorganized under the name of the Southern Pacific Company which was created by special act of the Legislature of Kentucky on March 17, 1884. In 1887, the Southern Pacific purchased the South Pacific Coast Railroad for a reported figure of $6,000,000 and inherited from the narrow gauge, among other things, the present-day emblem of the Southern Pacific Company depicting the track with the setting sun.

The purchase of the South Pacific Coast brought the ferry fleet now operating under one company up to thirteen boats, the *Alameda, Oakland, Encinal, Garden City, Bay City, Newark, Thoroughfare, Transit, Solano, El Capitan, Amador, Capital,* and the *Piedmont.* This last-named vessel was built by the Central Pacific and placed in service on November 28, 1883. Two hundred seventy feet long, the *Piedmont* was the only beamless beam engine boat on San Francisco Bay. Her remarkable engine, to be described in another chapter, had the longest piston stroke of any marine engine in the world — an unprecedented fourteen feet.

SOUTHERN PACIFIC PHOTO

The *Encinal,* fourth boat of the South Pacific Coast Railroad, unfurls her flags on a Sunday outing.

SOUTHERN PACIFIC PHOTO

The only boat on the Bay with a "beamless" beam engine, the *Piedmont* was a Southern Pacific veteran which carried the commuters for 56 years.

The first vessel to be built for the new Southern Pacific Company was the steel-hulled *Berkeley,* which was launched in 1898 by the Union Iron Works in San Francisco, famous builders of the battleship *Oregon,* the cruiser *Olympia,* and other noted ships of the "Great White Fleet." The *Berkeley* was a radical departure from the boats of walking beam and paddle wheel of the Central Pacific era. Her hull, instead of wood, was built of steel up to the main deck and her engine was a triple expansion, the type then in vogue for all ocean-going steamers built at that time. The line shafting of the *Berkeley* was coupled to both ends of the main engine crankshaft and this transmitted the power to two screw propellers, one at each end of the vessel. The *Berkeley* has withstood her fifty-four years of service in good shape, and, at the time of this writing, is still going strong.

On April 18, 1906, the famous earthquake hit San Francisco, followed by three days of raging fires. The ferryboats of the Southern Pacific rendered valiant service in transporting teams and passengers from the scene of the disaster and the crews worked long hours to aid in the relief of the stricken city. Passengers were carried free of charge as the railroad threw open its many facilities to the evacuees. Many of the rail routes had become so badly disrupted by the earthquake that the ferries served as one of the most effective and positive means of escape from the wreckage. No questions were asked if the destiny of the passenger were away from the city, but the patrol officers were very careful whom they let land. Two policemen were stationed at either side of the landing apron for screening purposes, and many drunks and looters were run back on board the vessel.

In recognition of the advent of the "horseless carriage," a vehicular ferry named the *Melrose* was built by the Southern Pacific in 1908, going into service on the Creek Route on January 11, 1909. In this same year, the first steamer *Thoroughfare* was broken up and a second vessel of the same name was built in 1912 as a companion for the *Melrose.* The two boats were somewhat alike, both being 294 feet long and being powered by better than 1,000 horsepower each. The birth of the auto ferry on San Francisco Bay was probably regarded as merely an experiment at the time and little thought was given to the future that might, and did bring a fleet of over thirty vessels devoted exclusively to the auto transport trade.

About this time, another radical change was effected in the Southern Pacific's local systems. Up to 1910, all the local trains had been operated in Oakland, Alameda, and Berkeley with steam power. However, the turn of the century saw the local steam lines begin to bow to a newcomer to the interurban and suburban railway field — the electric train.

In 1902, electrification of existing steam lines had begun in Marin County by the North Shore Railroad, while in 1903 the San Francisco & Oakland Terminal Railway had begun a local electric line competitive to the Southern Pacific's steam lines in the Oakland - Berkeley - Alameda area. The immediate public acceptance of the new mode in transit facilities was such that the Southern Pacific found it necessary to commence its own program of electrical conversion. In 1908 the steam lines began to see the weblike structure of the overhead trolley lines being strung out with final conversion taking place in 1913. At first the electric trains were operated as a division of the Southern Pacific, later termed the East Bay Electric Division and operated under the same book of rules as mainline steam trains with the head-end man being called an engineer rather than a motorman, as on the S.F.&O.T. Ry. In 1930 operation of the trains was taken over by a wholly-owned subsidiary of the Southern Pacific known as the Interurban Electric Railway. The "Red Trains," as the S.P. electric trains were called by those who rode them, continued to operate over the San Francisco - Oakland Bay Bridge even after the local ferry service had been discontinued to Oakland Pier, with only connecting service being provided by ferry for mainline passengers destined to Overland Route, Shasta Route, San Joaquin Valley Route, and Sacramento local passengers from San Francisco's Ferry Building.

But even the Interurban Electric felt the pinch two years later as parallel Key Route trains and buses drew more and more business from the I.E., although schedules and rates were identical. "The Key," however, had installed ultramodern, semistreamlined equipment in its train service and operated a superior type of motor coach on its Oakland - San Francisco coach runs, and this more comfortable equipment may have been the deciding factor.

The first ferryboat with propeller drive was the *Berkeley*, built by the Union Iron Works in 1898. Her triple expansion engine still throbs in her steel hull as this Southern Pacific ferry plies between the Ferry Building and Oakland Pier.

Southern Pacific Shipyard in Oakland about 1910. The ferryboats *Melrose* and *Newark* are tied up along with other Bay craft; the mouth of the Estuary, Alameda wharf and the Western Pacific Mole are visible in the distance.

Returning now to the earlier days of the Southern Pacific ferry operation, let us resume with the retirement in 1914 of Captain John Leale from the S.P. ferry service. It seems quite fitting to relate here the last trip on the eve of a ferry captain's retirement, not only to illustrate the sentiment some of the men had for their ships but equally to show the affection and loyalty the crews and commuters alike held for the men who guided their ships across the Bay since infancy. We are fortunate enough to have the Captain's own statement of the event and it is interesting to note that the last vessel of his command was the *Newark,* the same ship that he had commissioned thirty-seven years before.

"It is the last day of May, 1914," stated Captain Leale. "As I go on duty this Sunday morning, I have a feeling that it is to be a tame windup, for the regular commuters will be missing. At any rate, the *Newark* is an old friend, and I am a bit sentimental as the fact comes to mind that at my first and last trips as captain, I am in command of what is considered the finest ferryboat on the Bay. Five p.m. and my last trip from the City, and nothing unusual to indicate it.

"Half an hour later I left Oakland Pier homeward bound, starting the boat as usual from the shore end. As I walked the hurricane deck toward the other pilot-house, the fog bell on the end of the pier began to ring, the company's fire tug *Ajax,* lying at Outer Wharf, commenced blowing her whistle, and on entering the pilot-house, I was greeted by my friends, Allan Pollock, Judge Melvin, my brother, 'Bill,' and my worthy successor, Captain

John Carson. After a handshake all around, we were meeting the *Piedmont* with her flags flying and whistle blowing and crew lined up on the hurricane deck. As we met the other boats in crossing, each saluted with her whistle. The result was that we were busy answering three blasts all the way over. I took the helm and made the landing with a quiet resolve not to break a pile. After I 'rang her off,' I went down on deck where a delegation of company employees and other friends who had come on board were awaiting me to offer congratulations."

Any story of Southern Pacific steamer operation would be incomplete if no mention was made of the Southern Pacific's shipyard at West Oakland. Although the company had maintained a yard of one sort or another ever since it had been operating ferryboats, the modern yard with its marine railway was not available for repair work until 1902. One of the largest problems of marine operation is the maintenance and repair of vessels. This work can be accomplished in three ways:

(1) Accomplish the repairs by using a ship's force during regular layup periods or on overtime; (2) accomplish all repairs not within the scope of the ship's force by contract with shipyards; (3) accomplish repairs at the yard or works of the steamship operator. The Southern Pacific chose the latter alternative for its repairs after the turn of the century, the fleet being large enough to warrant the sustaining of a continuously operated yard. Assistant Superintendent of the Ferry Fleet Charles Green was for many

SOUTHERN PACIFIC PHOTO

Second boat of the name, the giant *Contra Costa* shared the Port Costa - Benicia train crossing with the *Solano*. Built in 1914, she was not as successful as her companion. After the cessation of service, the hull was rebuilt into three large barges.

years the principal figure in the S.P. Shipyard, and, during his day, many new vessels and modernization of old ships was accomplished at the yard.

The first vessel to be completely constructed by the shipyard was the *Melrose*, in 1908, no small ship at 2,662 gross tons. The second effort was second *Thoroughfare*, built in 1912, a boat similar to the *Melrose*. Following these two ships came the second *Alameda*, the *Santa Clara*, and the second *Contra Costa*. Although the *Contra Costa* could not be classed the same as the other two vessels, nevertheless the three of them were built very closely together and represented a new machinery design in marine engines. The power plants were the product of the company's shops in Sacramento and were a locomotive engineer's idea of what a marine engine should look like. Each vessel had two compound engines which were in no way connected together, each engine driving one paddle wheel on each side of the boat. This feature improved the maneuverability of the craft, something required more on the *Contra Costa* than on the other two because she was used in conjunction with the *Solano* on Carquinez Straits, ferrying trains across to the Solano County shore from the Contra Costa side. It may be of interest to note here that for many years the Southern Pacific Railroad used locomotives no larger than the 2400 class on the Western Division, the answer lying in the ferryboats, for the 2400 class were the largest locomotives which could ride the decks of the *Solano* and the *Contra Costa*.

The *Contra Costa* was the largest vessel ever built at the S.P. Shipyard, being 433 feet long and being admeasured at 5,373 gross tons. Her two engines developed a combined 3,000 horsepower, an amount never equalled on San Francisco Bay by any other ferry of the sidewheel variety. The *Contra Costa* had eight boilers, four on each side, and these, when added to the weight of the engines, concentrated a large part of the heavier members of the boat far off centerline on both the port and starboard sides of the vessel. This weight concentration tended to cause the boat to try to split herself in two. To arrest this defect, added structural tiebars had to be installed. Although a constant source of trouble to the sixteen years of the boat's life, the stress and strain had nothing to do with the decision to terminate the boat's active service which came to an end, together with that of the *Solano*, on November 30, 1930, when the tiny locomotive, the *C. P. Huntington*, Southern Pacific Locomotive Number One, crossed Carquinez Straits on the new S.P. Bridge which, when opened for traffic, spelled the end of a service which began back in 1879.

The *Alameda*, built in 1913, and the *Santa Clara*, built in 1914, were used in ferry service between San Francisco and Oakland or Alameda. The ships had steel hulls, their engines operated at a higher number of revolutions per minute than those of the average paddle-wheel boat, and those orange-colored wheels really used to "whizz" around. Built in similar fashion to the *Contra Costa*, with machinery outboard, a huge runway the length of the vessel permitted a large amount of mainline baggage and express to be hauled every trip.

In 1920 the shipyard undertook a modernization program of the ferry-

The ferryboat *Santa Clara*, together with her sister, the *Alameda*, were two of the few two-stacked boats of San Francisco Bay. After a lengthy service for the Southern Pacific, they were used to serve the shipyards during the war and were finally scrapped about 1947.

SOUTHERN PACIFIC PHOTO

The *Alameda* enters the slip at Oakland Pier with her decks teeming with commuters. This picture was taken just prior to the cessation of local ferry service.

boats, the *Oakland* being the first vessel to be rebuilt. Old *Chrysopolis* was under the surgeon's knife again, this time for a few changes in the main engine structure, enlarging and refinishing of the upper deck cabin, and the installation throughout of more spacious windows in continuing rows located on both decks. And after the carpenters and joiners got through with her, they sent her off on another twenty-year tour of duty on San Francisco Bay.

By 1907 the Southern Pacific had acquired financial interest in the Northwestern Pacific Railroad Company, operators of the Sausalito and Tiburon ferries, and two of the N.W.P. boats were rebuilt at the yard. The work on the *Sausalito* was not so far reaching as the tremendous rebuilding job accomplished on the *Ukiah,* which was stripped in 1920 and rebuilt as the steamer *Eureka,* completed in 1922. Although some machinery and structure was salvaged, the *Ukiah* was all but demolished with the result that the resultant *Eureka* was practically a new vessel.

Next on the agenda was the dismantling of Captain Leale's old ferry, the *Newark.* Having started life as a 294-footer, the *Newark* had been rebuilt and the over-all length shortened to 276 feet. She was hauled out for rebuilding February 18, 1901, and returned to service August 14, 1902. The tremendous paddle wheels which distinguished the ship from the other ferries, above all other features, had been cut down in size and the engine centers had been changed to compensate for this alteration. Smaller wheels were not such ungainly structures and the maneuverability of the boat was

Carrying the last train across Carquinez Straits on November 30, 1930, the *Solano* ended her reign in one of the most unique ferry services in the world.

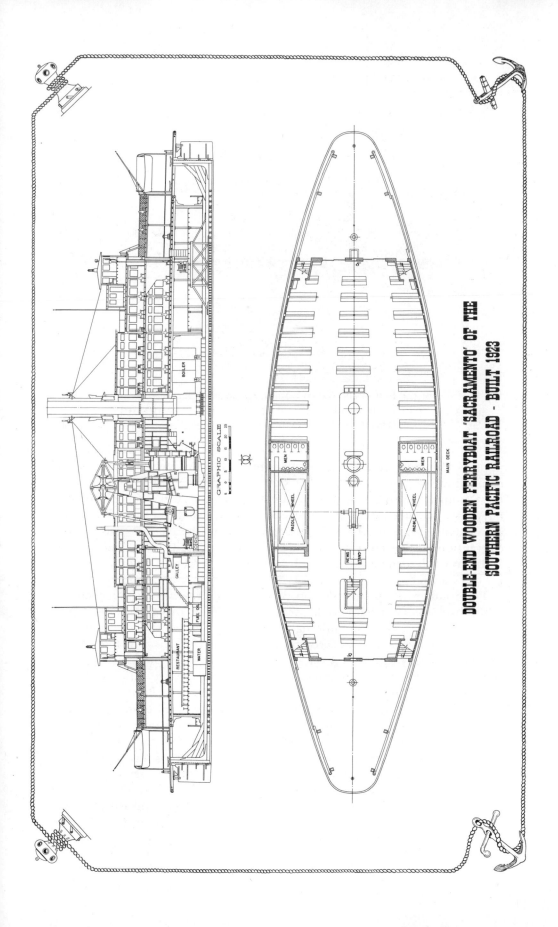

DOUBLE-END WOODEN FERRYBOAT 'SACRAMENTO' OF THE
SOUTHERN PACIFIC RAILROAD - BUILT 1923

GRAPHIC SCALE
5 0 5 10 15 20 25

MAIN DECK

MEN

MEN

MENS BIND

PADDLE WHEEL

PADDLE WHEEL

BOILER

GALLEY

FUEL OIL

RESTAURANT

WATER

Built out of the hull of the *Newark,* the large steamer *Sacramento* entered the passenger service of the Southern Pacific in 1923, and still carries mainline passengers from San Francisco to Oakland Pier.

improved, besides facilitating repair work. The big wheels put such a momentous way on the vessel that she was very awkward to stop, and, if there is anything that fails to be an asset to its owners, it's an unstoppable ferryboat! Besides battering down ferry slips, it usually inflicted considerable damage to itself. After the 1902 conversion, the *Newark* had a more conventional appearance but the wood frames and planking had worked and warped to such an extent that by 1921 either a rebuilding or a breaking up was inevitable.

The Southern Pacific decided on the former alternative and the resultant rebuilding was even more widespread than that of the *Ukiah.* The proverbial feat of major shipbuilding, "jacking up the whistle and sliding a new boat underneath," was accomplished, and in 1923 the new ferry *Sacramento,* with only fifty feet of the *Newark's* keel in her structure, slid down the ways at the S.P. yard, the finest ferry in the Southern Pacific fleet. The *Sacramento* was the last ferryboat built for the Southern Pacific and, be it noted, even at this late date the old tried and true vertical beam engine was used for the new ship. In many respects, the *Sacramento* resembled the *Eureka,* both vessels being close to 300 feet in length. The *Sacramento* could seat 1,900 persons, having the largest seating capacity of any boat in the fleet, thus making the vessel ideal for peak-load commuter service.

Last of the vessels to be converted at the yard was the *Piedmont* which was modernized and altered mechanically in 1923. The modernization for the most part consisted of a conversion similar to that performed on the *Oakland.*

With such large ferries as the *Sacramento, Santa Clara, Alameda, Oakland, Berkeley,* and the *Piedmont,* the old *Bay City* and *Garden City* were retired to the Vallejo - Vallejo Junction run and were finally removed from service in 1929 with the completion of the Carquinez highway bridge. *El Capitan* had enjoyed her final days of service on this route, being retired in 1921. The boats of the old era, the favorites of the Eighties, had given way to the larger vessels which could handle the increasing traffic on a heavily traveled Oakland ferry. In 1930, the S.P. passenger boats carried nearly twenty million persons.

Between 1922 and 1927, the Southern Pacific built nine automobile ferryboats, all constructed at private yards, and all to be dealt with in another chapter. These nine boats plus the second *Thoroughfare* were eventually transferred in 1929 to a separate corporation engaged solely in the operation of auto ferries.

The San Francisco - Oakland Bay Bridge was opened to electric train traffic, January 15, 1939, and the Interurban Electric Railway rerouted the "Red Trains" from Oakland Mole to the East Bay Terminal in San Francisco on this date. The day previous, January 14, the Southern Pacific operated their ferries on the last commuter runs between San Francisco and Oakland. The *Piedmont* and the *Oakland* were soon declared surplus boats, although they were rented on occasion to the Key System for operation to the World's Fair on Treasure Island in the summer of 1939.

The *Alameda* and the *Santa Clara* were extra boats and the mainline passengers and baggage were carried on the *Berkeley,* the *Sacramento,* and later on the *Eureka* after the abandonment of the Northwestern Pacific's Sausalito service.

The commuters were sentimental about their ferries, and gave them up reluctantly as they bowed toward inevitable "progress." The Alameda commuters felt so strongly on the matter that they considered a municipal ferry as an answer to their problems. But all the arguments that were brought forth resulted in little action and the ferries gave the proverbial inch in the battle with the bridges.

The Wakemans, the Minturns, and the others who commenced San Francisco Bay ferry operation are now names among the departed and the Bay they navigated has changed materially since the first ferryboat plied its waters. But that change stemmed from the good old days of yore when the riverboat conquered the Bay.

Chapter III

FROM PADDLE WHEELS TO PROPELLERS

THE CENTRAL PACIFIC and its successor, the Southern Pacific, did not enjoy a complete monopoly in the East Bay ferry traffic. The serious competition did not begin until the turn of the century but when it came, no less than two transcontinental rail lines and one local electric line whittled away at the Southern Pacific's heretofore unrivaled operation.

The competitors respected the judgment of their historic rival and in two cases their conquest of the Bay was commenced in a similar fashion. Riverboats, this time from the Columbia River, were brought in to inaugurate the service. This was partly due to the fact that no ferryboats were available on the local market. All that could run or were worth fixing up were pressed into the service of the Southern Pacific. New boats were an expensive commodity, delivery dates were uncertain, so the cheaper alternative of purchasing second-hand vessels was resorted to.

First of the rival companies to reach San Francisco Bay was the Santa Fe. This road, in 1895, was operating from Chicago to Los Angeles and San Diego, and had come as far north as Mojave in eastern Southern California. On February 20 of the same year a group of capitalists from the towns of the San Joaquin Valley organized the independent San Francisco & San Joaquin Railway. The group, headed by Claus Spreckels, a railroad magnate in his own right as builder of the narrow-gauge Pajaro Valley Consolidated Railway, raised considerable cash on short notice, hired William B. Storey, later president of the Santa Fe, as chief engineer, and started to build. Storey had considerable railroad experience, having worked extensively on the Southern Pacific's Shasta Route during its construction, and he enjoyed quite a reputation as a railroad builder.

The new road commenced building at Stockton, for this San Joaquin River town enjoyed the convenience of deep water, and the shippers could freight by rail to this terminus from whence the goods could be transferred to ships and carried by vessels to San Francisco and any other port of the world. In 1896 the line was opened to Fresno while 1898 found the rails as far south as Bakersfield. A new grade over the Tehachapi Mountains was then considered impossible of construction so, in order to scale the mountain ramparts which lay between the termini of Bakersfield and Mojave, the San Francisco & San Joaquin built a bit further south of Bakersfield to

The first boat of the Santa Fe Railway was the *Ocean Wave*, built in Portland, Oregon, in 1891. She inaugurated the San Francisco - Richmond ferry service in 1900.

Kern Junction where their rails joined those of the Southern Pacific and the two roads used the S.P.'s trackage over the Tehachapis by mutual agreement. At Mojave, the S.F.&S.J. connected with the Santa Fe, which, by this time had acquired the valley line.

The Atchison, Topeka & Santa Fe bravely started life in the Sixties with programs and promises which no one thought would ever be fulfilled. But its promoters had faith, worked hard, played their cards wisely, and all but spanned the continent in thirty years' time. When the Santa Fe got control of the San Francisco & San Joaquin Railway, nothing could stop it. Stockton was too close to San Francisco. The Santa Fe would close the gap and finally make true Colonel Holliday's promise of a continuous rail line from Chicago to San Francisco, all under the ownership of one company.

The track was built from Stockton, through tule swamps and river lands, across Franklin Canyon, and down to the Bay of San Francisco at last, the railroad ending its cross-country trail at the deep-water port of Richmond, California, where a ferry line would carry on to San Francisco. Such progress was made by the new transcontinental line that the Point Richmond terminal was reached in advance of schedule and the railroad was beginning to grow desperate for a passenger ferry.

W. A. Bissell, traffic manager of the Santa Fe, was acquainted with Captain John Leale of the Southern Pacific Company's ferry fleet. One day he said, "Jack, we have to start operations to Point Richmond very soon and we haven't time to build a boat. There is nothing in these waters to suit.

What's the matter with your getting a month's vacation and going up north and seeing what you can find?"

Captain Leale said he would be very happy to look around if the Santa Fe could make the necessary arrangements with his employers, the Southern Pacific. At this point, it might be interesting to note that, although highly competitive in the traffic field, Southern Pacific and Santa Fe were almost happily co-operative in the operating department during their pioneering days, something that has resulted beneficially for all the West since it enabled both systems to develop the areas of California which they served, whether exclusively or jointly. Thus, we have noted the Southern Pacific agreeing to a joint trackage arrangement over the Tehachapis; next, a Southern Pacific ferry captain is permitted to go search for a suitable boat for his rival; and later, when the Northwestern Pacific Railroad is to be formed, we will find the Santa Fe and the Southern Pacific working together to bring about the merger of the various lines, some of which had been built by one road, others by the other, until finally the network was knit into one system serving the Redwood Empire.

And so the Southern Pacific gave Captain Leale his vacation and the post-man took off on his holiday. First to Portland, then to Seattle and Tacoma, where the captain met Cary W. Cook, who took him to Vancouver, British Columbia, and then to New Westminster on the Fraser River. Cook had the steamer *Ocean Wave* for sale. The *Ocean Wave* was a fine little vessel, having been designed by Jacob Kamm for the Ilwaco Railway & Transportation Company, a narrow-gauge railway system in Washington, and built in Portland, Oregon, in 1891. She was a sidewheel steamer admeasuring 724 gross tons, being 180 feet long between perpendiculars, and having a 29-foot moulded beam with a registered depth of nine feet.

The ship was admirably built with two passenger decks, two masts and high paddle boxes. Entirely of wood construction, the heavy frames and planking of the vessel rendered her an extremely sturdy craft and Captain Leale bought her for his own account on condition that she could turn her wheel over with her own steam on arrival in San Francisco. She had fifty staterooms on her main deck and a hundred on her upper deck, all of which had to be torn up to make way for the luxurious saloon.

The *Ocean Wave* left Port Angeles in the tow of the tug *Holyoke* on Saturday evening, May 20, 1899, boarded up against the sea and ballasted with water. The seas were calm during the passage, however, and the single-ender arrived in San Francisco without mishap on May 24. The Santa Fe terminal company then made out its first check, the recipient being John Leale who had just sold the company the steamer *Ocean Wave*.

Newly painted, with the cross-circle-square emblem of the Santa Fe gracing her paddle boxes and polished to within an inch of her nautical life, the graceful steamer *Ocean Wave* stood fast in her slip at the Ferry Building in San Francisco the morning of July 6, 1900. Captain Lauritzen was on the bridge, Chief Engineer Ed Mahoney was at the throttle, and the little steamer throbbed in readiness for the momentous occasion. Promptly at

The powerful little *San Pablo* was a familiar sight for over thirty years of operation between Richmond and the Ferry Building. Built at the Union Iron Works,
her 2,000 horsepower was tops in its day.

8:00 a.m. the engine-room telegraph rattled its alarum bell, the paddle
wheels began to turn, and the *Ocean Wave* moved out upon the Bay. The
trip from the Ferry Building to Point Richmond took forty minutes, at the
end of which time the little steamer docked, passengers and baggage were
made safe aboard the train, and the locomotive engineer whistled off. The
Ocean Wave whistled back a salute and the first transcontinental train from
Richmond over Santa Fe rails all the way rolled east to Chicago.

Although the *Ocean Wave* made Santa Fe history, her light engines were
unsuitable for the heavy Richmond run. The railroad was quick to recog-
nize this fact and therefore ordered a new boat which was more suitable
for their operation. Designed by F. B. King, the successful bidder to build
the ship was the Union Iron Works. The vessel was 226 feet long, had a
beam over the guards of sixty-four feet and was admeasured at 1,584 gross
tons. The new vessel was christened the *San Pablo* and was placed in service
late in 1900 to become the principal ferryboat of the Santa Fe. The vessel
had two decks and was double ended. Her engine was an inclined marine
compound, steam being generated therefor by four boilers. The engine
drove two 16-foot paddlewheels and both the paddlewheels and hull were
of steel construction, a radical departure in ferryboat building at the time.

The Santa Fe continued to operate for about ten years with the two boats
but, as business increased and the *Ocean Wave* grew older, need for another

ferry was recognized. The satisfaction reflected in the experience of the railroad with the *San Pablo* influenced the design of the newly proposed ferry which was very similar in hull details, the only essential mechanical difference being the valve gear on the main engine. Again the Union Iron Works was the builder and in 1911 the new ferry steamer *San Pedro* was delivered to the Santa Fe. The new ship was ?? feet longer than the *San Pablo* and the length was added at the extremes. The *San Pablo* had been a trifle too short and her natural wake built up a swell in the way of the paddle wheels which reduced the effectiveness of the buckets. The twin vessel to the *San Pablo* had been the North Pacific Coast Railway's *Tamalpais* and her owners had made this change in length in the latter vessel within but a few months after she was built. The *Tamalpais* then became the most efficient vessel of the pair and so the lines of the *San Pedro* were copied from the revamped *Tamalpais*. The *San Pedro* was bristling with power, as her four Babcock & Wilcox boilers delivered an indicated 2,000 horsepower to her inclined poppet valve engine. The *"Pedro"* was one of the finest passenger ferries ever to ply the waters of San Francisco Bay — a distinguished looking boat with her two stacks, one ahead of the other, pouring out the black smoke as the white wake of her paddles disappeared in the distance. Both the *San Pedro* and the *San Pablo* were coal-burning ships when originally built but were converted to oil burners while operating for the Santa Fe.

With the two double-ended ferries in regular service, the steamer *Ocean Wave* was retired in 1911 and moored by the railroad company at Antioch, California. Later, Captain Leale, her original purchaser for the Santa Fe's account, again bought her with the intention of scrapping her. But the first World War was then on and the *Ocean Wave* was again reprieved when the Shipping Board bought her from Leale in 1917 for the purpose of making her a receiving ship for the Sea Training Service. Her engines were removed to provide more space for barracks and for a period of about three and a half years she served as housing for the trainees awaiting merchant ships. Sold again to a floating restaurant operator, she gradually disintegrated as do all old hulls, and another pioneer passed from the picture.

The Richmond - San Francisco passenger ferry operation of the Santa Fe plodded along for over twenty years after the building of the *San Pedro*. In the meantime, the Santa Fe had bought up the Oakland - East Richmond segment of a narrow-gauge railroad which had been planned by its owner-builder, "Borax" Smith, to run from Oakland to Death Valley, California, but which got as far east as Bryants (near what is now Orinda, California) despite its ambitious name of the California - Nevada Railway. The Santa Fe then built a connection from the Richmond depot east to a connection with the grade of the former California - Nevada line, relaid the latter to standard gauge, and completed the project into the Oakland terminal at Fortieth and San Pablo with the first train arriving on May 16, 1904. It was finally concluded that the Richmond operation was too costly for the benefit derived and an arrangement was finally concluded with the

The two stacked *San Pedro* was the pride of the Santa Fe fleet for 23 years. Her fine hull and engines, product of the Union Iron Works, continued to serve after the Santa Fe abandoned service, for the vessel was renamed *Treasure Island* and operated for the Key System, as shown below; in the ferry route to the World's Fair in 1939 and 1940.

Southern Pacific whereby the Santa Fe joined the former's mainline at the west end of the Santa Fe's Oakland yards at Chestnut Junction, operating over the Southern Pacific line to the Oakland Mole where terminal facilities were leased, including the ferry service operated by the S.P. This arrangement continued until the opening of the San Francisco - Oakland Bay Bridge in 1939 when the Santa Fe terminated their trains at the Fortieth and San Pablo station where San Francisco passengers were transferred to motor coaches at the trainside thence over the Bay Bridge to the Santa Fe Passenger Terminal at historic Pioneer Place, 44 Fourth Street.

So, on April 22, 1933, the *"Pedro"* and the *"Pablo"* banked their fires and another ferry route disappeared from the Bay. The two vessels remained at the Richmond wharf until 1937 when the *San Pablo* was scrapped and the *San Pedro* was sold to the Exposition Transportation Company to operate to the World's Fair on Treasure Island. The old two-funneled standby of the Santa Fe was renamed *Treasure Island* and operated by the Key System for the duration of the Golden Gate International Exposition in 1939 and 1940.

*　　　　*　　　　*　　　　*　　　　*　　　　*

Another encroacher on the Southern Pacific's transcontinental traffic was the Western Pacific Railroad which connected with the Denver & Rio Grande Western at Salt Lake City, Utah, to provide another route from San Francisco to the East. The Western Pacific actually carried out what had been the golden dream of the narrow-gauge South Pacific Coast Railroad some thirty years before, in that it connected with the D.&R.G.W. Things had changed quite a bit since the days of Fair's line, for the Denver & Rio Grande had converted much of its trackage to standard gauge and, with a connection at the western end of its line with the Western Pacific and at the eastern end with the Chicago, Burlington & Quincy, a new through route to Chicago was offered, the third of such routes to San Francisco.

The Western Pacific started its railroad building at a late date for the cream had been skimmed off the top by its predecessors and the running was rough after the turn of the century. In 1906 the railroad had built into Oakland, and from east and west the Utah Construction Company had pushed it through until on November 2, 1909, the last spike was driven at Keddie in the Feather River Canyon, from whence the railroad derived its trademark, a red feather.

The Western Pacific main line reached the Bay by skirting the Oakland shore of the Estuary and at the mouth of the creek a pier and wharf were built as a landing place for ferries and barges. Preliminary ferry operation prior to revenue service was commenced with rented Key System boats which made such an impression on the officials of the Western Pacific that the design of these vessels was followed by the Western Pacific when they built the one and only passenger ferryboat constructed originally for their own use at a later date.

Scouting around the Columbia River, company agents came across the sternwheelers *Telegraph* and *Telephone,* typical river vessels of the Oregon - Washington boundary stream. After considerable preliminary dickering, a satisfactory agreement for the purchase of the *Telephone* was arranged, together with the risky delivery of the vessel. The agents were able to get together a crew which was willing to sail the vessel from Portland, Oregon, to San Francisco under her own power. Although the venture seemed ill advised, the daring spirit of Captain Ned Wakeman and his *New World* must have kept watch and care of the coastwise plodding *Telephone* for she eventually steamed in through the Golden Gate intact, much to the joy of the Western Pacific.

The *Telephone* was built in Portland, Oregon, in 1903. She was 201 feet in length and was admeasured at 632 gross tons. Builders of both hull and engine remain a mystery and her timbers and castings were probably the remains of another vessel transplanted into the *Telephone,* for this was the custom of the riverboat builders. She had lots of power, and, after the shores and false bulkheads erected for the sea trip were removed, the churning sternwheeler was ready for the Western Pacific's passenger run. On August 22, 1910, she carried the first revenue passengers from the San Francisco Ferry Building to the Oakland terminal.

The *Telephone* soon set many speed records on San Francisco Bay. Because she was a sternwheel vessel, she had to back out of the pier at each end of the trip and execute a 180-degree turn before being able to get fully

First boat of the Western Pacific Railway was the sternwheeler *Telephone,* built in Portland, Oregon, in 1903. She initiated ferry service between San Francisco and the Western Pacific Oakland Mole in August, 1910.

MOULIN PHOTO

The launching of the ferryboat *Edward T. Jeffery* for the Western Pacific by Moore and Scott Iron Works, Oakland, on July 19, 1913. Below, the *Jeffery,* renamed *Feather River,* tied up at an Oakland wharf shortly before the discontinuance of Western Pacific Service.

under way. Paralleling the Southern Pacific route from the Ferry Building
to Oakland, an Espee boat starting at the same time as the *Telephone*
would be well under way before the sternwheeler had executed all of her
preliminary steps. Handicapped as she was, though, the *Telephone* would
"get up and git" once she was straightened out. Foot by foot, she would
catch up with the S.P. boat, the big orange sternwheel grinding away, the
flat-bottomed hull gliding across the windswept Bay. Soon the vessels
would be abreast — then the *Telephone* would pull away — and she never
lost a race. The *Telephone* was the last of the riverboats in San Francisco
Bay ferry service, but what she had in speed was not sufficient to overcome
the disadvantages of a riverboat on a bay. While executing her turning
maneuvers at each end of the voyage, the craft was in the nature of a men-
ace to navigation and there was a large amount of traffic up and down the
San Francisco waterfront in 1910. As previously mentioned, the Key System
type of ferry had taken the fancy of the Western Pacific officials and plans
were soon drawn up to secure a fast and practical double ender as soon as
possible.

Contracted for in 1912, the new ferryboat was built at the Moore & Scott
Iron Works in Oakland, the builders being a predecessor of the present
Moore Dry Dock Company. The little vessel was 218 feet long, had a
42-foot beam, and was admeasured at 1,578 gross tons. She was named for
the president of the Western Pacific at that time, Edward T. Jeffery, and
she was painted red with the "Feather River Route" emblem on her stack.
Amid much ceremony, she slid down the ways at Moore & Scott on July 19,
1913, and was placed in service very shortly thereafter. Her engines were
double compounds, two high-pressure and two low-pressure cylinders on
the same shaft. She was propeller-driven, having a continuous shaft driving
a forward and an after screw. Four watertube boilers generated steam for
the *Edward T. Jeffery* and the main engine developed 2,500 indicated horsepower. Almost as fast as the *Telephone*, the new vessel was very satisfactory in all respects and, from the day she was placed in service, single-hand-
edly she carried on the Western Pacific's ferry service until the end.

The *Telephone* was junked in 1918 after several years of inactivity. All
this time the *"Jeffrey"* ploughed on without incident, save for a changing
of her name to the more appropriate *Feather River* — or so the railroad's
advertising department reckoned. The new boat seated one thousand persons, but the railroad operated but one transcontinental passenger train a
day in each direction; so, with somewhat the same philosophy which
prompted the Santa Fe to give up the ferryboat ghost, the Western Pacific
also quit operating a ferry in 1933.

Also as the Santa Fe had done, arrangements were concluded with the
Southern Pacific to operate trains in and out of Oakland Pier. In exchange
for this privilege and for the carriage of Western Pacific passengers on
Southern Pacific ferryboats, the Western Pacific turned over the *Feather
River* to the S.P. to operate. This was in May, 1933, and the little ship
already burdened with names, had still another one hung on her, this time

the *Sierra Nevada*. Dubbed by her crews the *"Rocky Mountain,"* the *Sierra Nevada* carried on for the S.P., serving as a relief boat and pinchhitting on the Sausalito run for the Northwestern Pacific Railroad's ferry service. Despite her age, she could make the trip from Sausalito to the Ferry Building in twenty-two minutes while it took the Northwestern boats a full thirty-two minutes. She was loaned to the Key System during the 1939 fair, then served for the War Shipping Administration as a shipyard ferry during World War II. After the war, the scrap heap? Not the *Sierra Nevada!* The Richmond - San Rafael Ferry acquired her in 1947, rebuilt her into an auto ferry and, at this writing, she's still in service. Yes, it's safe to say that Moore & Scott built a truly fine boat when they built the *Edward T. Jeffrey*.

*   *   *   *   *   *

The most modern of all the ferryboat operators, the company with the most advanced ideas in both hull and engine design, was the Key System. From the title of this book, no record of the Key System rightfully belongs here for there were no paddle wheels in Key operation (on Key System - owned boats) and no walking beams ever rocked their lazy cadence on Key hurricane decks. Few operators of ocean-going vessels ever reached the stage of advancement of the Key System, and, when the chapter in national marine history is written on the development of the American ferryboat and its propulsion machinery, the Key System will take its rightful place at the head of the class.

From the beginning, "the Key" served notice that it thought little of paddle steamers. Up to the time that the Key System arrived on the transportation scene, there was but one screw propeller double-end ferryboat on the Bay, that being the S.P.'s *Berkeley*. The Southern Pacific had some hard luck with the ship at first for her propeller was not effective in arresting her way. The *Berkeley* became a notorious slip-destroying monster, and one of her captains once stated that it was necessary to close the throttle in the middle of the Bay in order to stop in time at the Ferry Building. While the Southern Pacific was trying to cope with the *Berkeley* and to solve the mystery of their marine juggernaut, the Key System was planning a fleet of similar boats, so convinced were they that the propeller steamers were the answer. But it would be best to start at the beginning.

Why was the Key System formed and what was its business? Incorporated in 1902, the San Francisco, Oakland & San Jose Railway was formed for the purpose of building a railway from Oakland to San Jose which would be electrically operated and which would commence at a terminal on San Francisco Bay with ferry service to the Ferry Building in San Francisco. Through much corporation-forming, financing, and all the accompanying headaches of getting a new enterprise started, the railroad began construction in 1902 of local electric trackage from a pier located on the shoalwaters of the Bay to uptown Oakland, Piedmont, and Berkeley, completion of the lines being accomplished in 1906, 1904, and 1903, respectively. The original layout, when traced on a map, appeared to resemble a key in many

ROBERT MCFARLAND PHOTO

The *San Jose* and the *Yerba Buena* were the first two boats of the Key System. The *San Jose* (above) made the first trip with passengers for the Key System, but the *Yerba Buena* (below) made the first trip with revenue passengers. Both boats were built by J. W. Dickie and were fitted with steam triple expansion engines for propulsion.

respects: The fingers of the pier being the unlatching prongs, the straight run of the track to the mainland the shank, and the lines to the cities of Berkeley, Piedmont and Oakland being the bow or handle of the key. So, no matter what corporate name was attached to the company, it was always known as the "Key Route," right from its earliest beginnings, and the popular name held long enough to eventually be changed to the Key System Transit Company in later years.

The operation of the Key System was in direct competition to the Southern Pacific local lines in the East Bay area which were then steam operated. In Bay railway operation, as noted before, only the North Shore Railroad in Marin County had started electric interurban railway construction at an earlier date, although the Key was the first to place electric trains in operation in regular service.

Immediately upon starting construction work on the rail line, the San Francisco, Oakland & San Jose Railway formed an affiliated corporation, the San Francisco & Oakland Terminal Railway, which planned and contracted for two ferryboats for use on the company's route from their Oakland Wharf to the Ferry Building in San Francisco. Builder and designer of the vessels was John W. Dickie whose yard was located in Alameda on the Estuary. The ships were named the *San Jose,* after the proposed southern terminus of the road, and the *Yerba Buena*, this being the Spanish name for San Francisco. The *Yerba Buena* should not be confused with the second vessel of that name which was operated by the Key System until service was discontinued and which later became a troop-carrying ferry for the Army's Transportation Corps.

The *San Jose* and the *Yerba Buena* were 175 feet long between perpendiculars and were approximately 700 gross tons. Powered by three-cylinder, triple-expansion engines driving propellers at both ends of the vessel, the little 1,200 horsepower ships were very efficient little ferryboats. The *Yerba Buena* was completed in August, 1903, with the *San Jose* having been built slightly earlier. With their orange paint and bristling with ventilators, the two ferries were ready for service before there was any traffic to handle. So, on September 24, 1903, the *San Jose* took a party of guests on a trial cruise just to demonstrate how splendid would be the service of the San Francisco & Oakland Terminal Railway. She performed beautifully but failed to get the nomination to make the inaugural commercial run. That honor fell to her sister craft, the *Yerba Buena,* and she, with Captain William A. Rasmussen at the helm and Chief Engineer August Mausshardt at the throttle, began the Key System's thirty-six year ferry stand on October 26, 1903.

From the first, business was booming. Although they had two boats, the San Francisco & Oakland Terminal Railway ran only one during the first month. But it was well that the company had ordered two boats because traffic was so brisk that on November 8, 1903, the railway began running two boats and by November 28 of the same year, the trips were operated on a twenty-minute schedule. The Key Route had chosen a very practical location for their pier in Oaland and the length of the run was a little less than three miles. However, the SOS went out for more boats and in 1904 the railway company again contracted with John Dickie for a third but larger vessel. The new ship was equipped with a double two-cylinder compound engine with both engines connected to the same shaft. This was the first engine of its kind for use on ferryboats on San Francisco Bay, and it proved itself sufficiently to be used on three other screw-propeller vessels built later, two of them Key Route boats and one being the Western Pacific's *Edward T. Jeffrey*. The advantage of this type of engine over the triple expansion type used on the first two ships was the fact that with two high pressure cylinders set at ninety degrees on the crankshaft, the engine could never get stuck on center, a most valuable feature when docking the boat. No matter what position the engine assumed when stopped, it could be started instantly without the use of a none-too-satisfactory bypass from the high pressure valve to the intermediate pressure valve as is the case in a triple expansion engine.

Launched in 1905 with a trial trip on April 5, the 2,000-horsepower *San Francisco* was the first in a series of bold mechanical steps taken by the Key Route. In 1907, John Dickie built two more vessels for the railway, both ships still larger in hull dimensions than the *San Francisco* although having an identical power plant. These were the *Fernwood*, made ready in November, 1907, and the *Claremont*, her predecessor by a few months. The orange fleet was now at full strength for the first time, and it remained at these five boats until 1919 when the *San Jose* was sold to the Six-Minute

ROBERT MCFARLAND PHOTO

The *San Francisco* (above) and her sisters, the *Claremont* and the *Fernwood* were the larger of the early Key System ferries. Their double compound engines were unique in design and gave the wooden ferries a wealth of power.

Ferry, operating across Carquinez Straits, and converted to an auto ferry for that service. It may be well to state here that the Key Route was the only exclusive passenger ferry system on the Bay and at no time did Key boats ever carry automobiles between San Francisco and Oakland.

In addition to its own electric empire, the Key Route became affiliated with the Oakland, Antioch & Eastern Railway which later developed into the San Francisco - Sacramento Railroad and finally wound up as the Sacramento Northern Railway which operated an electric interurban line from Oakland to Chico, hauling both freight and passengers. The passengers were handled by the Key ferries from San Francisco to the Key Pier where they boarded the shiny black Sacramento Northern trains. After leaving the Oakland city limits, the railroad wound through the hills in back of Piedmont, through Redwood Canyon, past St. Mary's College at Moraga, Walnut Creek and Concord, and eventually reached the Bay again, this time in the vicinity of Pittsburg. A crossing was necessary in order to continue with the trackage to Sacramento and a bridge crossing would have been too expensive since it would have had to include a movable span to permit the passage of vessels destined to Upper Bay points and those on the Sacramento and San Joaquin rivers. As an alternative, therefore, a car ferry was employed, the first such being a small boat named the *Bridgit,* later succeeded by the *Ramon,* a gasoline driven car ferry which was built in Pittsburg in 1914.

This unusual vessel, which is still in operation hauling the freight trains of the Sacramento Northern, is 203 feet long, has a beam of 40 feet, and a gross tonnage of 775 tons. Her gasoline engines develop 500 indicated horsepower on screw propellers. The *Ramon* suffers from the lack of flexibility demonstrated by the Southern Pacific's *Solano* and *Contra Costa,* sometimes having difficulty crossing upper Suisun Bay against a heavy wind or tide. One of her unique features is the series of overhead trolley lines on the vessel's single deck to accommodate the pantagraph or trolley-pole current pickup of the locomotives.

In the early Twenties, the Key Route found itself faced with the problem of obtaining new boats. And the prosperity of the ferry business was reflected in local shipyards, for, at the time the Union Iron Works was turning out six auto ferries for the Southern Pacific, Moore Dry Dock was rebuilding the *Cazadero* for the Northwestern Pacific, James Robertson was building the *City of Richmond* for the Richmond - San Rafael Ferry, and the same firm was also building the *Golden Gate* for the Golden Gate Ferry. The Dickie Brothers had passed from the picture and General Engineering was not yet ready for such an enterprise as building a ferryboat. Thus, when a new set of boats was to be built, the successful bidder was the Los Angeles Shipbuilding & Drydock Company in San Pedro, California.

The vessels were built in 1923, one being named the *Hayward* and completed in March, the other the *San Leandro* being made available in July. The vessels were 240 feet in length and had an over-all beam of 62 feet 7 inches. The depth of the hull was 19 feet 6 inches and the loaded draft

The *Hayward* (above) and the *San Leandro* (below) were two of the most advanced ferryboats in design in the world when built. Powered by General Electric turboelectric machinery, these two vessels, the product of Los Angeles Shipbuilding Company, were the smoothest riding ferryboats on San Francisco Bay.

was 11 feet 6 inches. The gross tonnage for the two steel hulls when completed was 1,653 tons.

The propulsion machinery for the two vessels was a new departure for ferryboats. It consisted of turboelectric drive, the machinery being manufactured by the General Electric Company. The vessels were of the first to use turboelectric direct current drive, there having been three vessels built in New York harbor previously which used turboelectric alternating current drive. The boiler plant consisted of two Babcock & Wilcox water tube boilers having a total heating surface of 5,000 square feet and a steam pressure of 225 pounds per square inch. The boilers were equipped with superheaters giving 65 degrees of superheat. The turbogenerator unit consisted of a three-stage Curtis type steam turbine connected through a single four-to-one reduction gear to a 1,000-kilowatt direct current generator. The generator gave a full load current of 2,000 amperes at 500 volts. The unit was a six-pole shunt wound machine, so designed that it had considerable overload capacity for short periods.

The two propulsion motors were located at opposite ends of the boat and were direct coupled to the two independent propeller shafts. It was this feature which increased the efficiency of the turboelectric boat nearly nineteen per cent, for the stern or driving motor could turn over at 125 revolutions per minute. The increased resistance of the forward propeller operating at full speed and the power required to drive a shaft the length of the ferryboat was thus eliminated by the turboelectric drive boats as compared to the triple expansion engine and the two cylinder compound types. Two armatures were located on the same shaft, the reason for this being that if the armature were not doubled, it would have produced too large a diameter motor, too large to place it as far aft as is possible with the double armature type.

When the *Hayward* was completed, more eyes than those of the Key System and the General Electric Company were focused on its propulsion plant. Would turboelectric drive prove practical for the ferryboat? And what about the passenger who would ride the Key Route turboelectric ferry while alongside him the beam engine paddle boats of the Southern Pacific would roll along, and the question would be asked, "Which one is best? If the turbine is so good, why do they stick to paddle wheels?' '

In the spring of 1923, the *Hayward* steamed out of Los Angeles Harbor with the Key Route experts, the General Electric engineers, and a few other observers watching her gauges and meters as she rolled up the Coast to the Golden Gate. The trip was a rough one and not without its anxious moments, but the *Hayward* came through and inaugurated turboelectric drive ferry service on San Francisco Bay, September 29, 1923. From the outset, the Key System was very satisfied with their new boat and she and her sister, the *San Leandro*, proved tops for riding qualities on the Oakland run.

Spurred on by their turboelectric successes, the walking beam and paddle wheel were definitely doomed in the Key Route world, and the company

MOULIN PHOTO

The ill-fated *Peralta*, together with her sister, the *Yerba Buena*, represented the finest in ferryboats when built. But a temporary bow submergence and a disastrous fire finished her career after a brief six years. She now sails on Puget Sound as the *Kalahala*.

again began planning new boats. The *San Francisco, Fernwood,* and *Claremont* were becoming too small for the Key's commuter traffic and even the *Hayward* and *San Leandro* would have been more efficient in revenue production had they been of greater passenger capacity.

Thus, two new boats were planned and these were to be all-steel hulls and superstructure, another radical departure in ferry construction. Even the *Hayward* and *San Leandro* were of wooden construction above the main deck level except in the case of main strength members. But the new plans called for all-steel vessels, again with turboelectric drive and featuring a synchronized forward and after rudder which made the vessels exceptionally easy to steer. Much water had passed over the dam since the days of the *Newark* and her four men on the manual wheels!

The new vessels were built by Moore Dry Dock Company of Oakland, the *Peralta* being delivered March 15, 1927, and the *Yerba Buena* (the second vessel of that name) being delivered the following month. The propulsion machinery was built by Westinghouse and consisted of a main generator and two propulsion motors which were arranged in similar fashion to the installation on the *Hayward* and *San Leandro*, developing 2,600 indicated horsepower. Steam was furnished by four Babcock & Wilcox water tube boilers, two located aft of the main generator and two forward of it. It has never been decided whether the designers of the vessels were really trying to be confusing or just accidentally hit upon it, but the *Peralta* and the *Yerba Buena* were double-end ferryboats in every sense of the word —

without exception. Everything that appeared at one end was duplicated at the other — symmetry was perfect and complete. According to Howard Hickman, port engineer for the Key Route, the company distinguished between the two ends merely by painting in one wheel-house the legend "Oakland End" and in the other, "San Francisco End."

The 2,000 gross ton vessels, 256 feet long and 68 feet in breadth over the guards, were placed in service in the late spring of 1927. At that time, the *San Francisco, Fernwood,* and *Claremont* were leased to the Golden Gate Ferry and were rebuilt as auto ferries even as the first *Yerba Buena* had been in 1924. The fine new ferries with their modern appointments and plate glass windows looked rather inharmonious alongside the Southern Pacific's *Sacramento, Oakland,* and their sister ferries with their walking beams and paddle wheels. But the newcomers were no finer in their day than the *New World* had been in hers and the shade of the *Chrysopolis* was heard to murmur that she too had been pretty — when young.

The orange turboelectric fleet set out to make a record on San Francisco Bay but a black sheep loomed up on the family horizon. The designers of the *Peralta* and *Yerba Buena* had tried to second-guess the commuters and had placed a large salt-water ballast tank at each end of the vessels. The after tank was always kept in ballast so that the crowd surging toward the forward end of the vessel would not materially affect its trim. A huge centrifugal pump in the engine room transferred this ballast while the vessel lay in the slip at each terminal. But the *Peralta* had the misfortune of having the *forward* tank in ballast on February 17, 1928, and when the crowd surged to the foredeck to await the landing, the bow dipped under and thirty persons were washed overboard, five of them being drowned.

This tragic occurrence led to the prompt discontinuance of the use of the ballast tanks and no further trouble of this sort developed. But on May 6, 1933, the Key System terminal and wharves in Oakland caught fire, the conflagration being of unknown origin but highly destructive. The *Peralta* was tied to the slip at the time and thus was enveloped by the flames and completely gutted. Service to the Oakland wharf was discontinued for three days while the Key System made repairs to the pier, but the *Peralta* suffered damage which would take considerable time and money to repair. As Artemus Ward would have put it, "this wuz 2 mutch."

Although reluctant to let the vessel go, the Key Route sold her to the Puget Sound Navigation Company in Seattle, Washington, and the latter company rebuilt the *Peralta* in 1935, rechristening her the *Kalakala*. The vessel was converted into a single-ender, considerably streamlined, and repowered with 3,000-horsepower Busch-Sulzer Brothers diesel engines. Flying the company flag of the Black Ball Line, she is still running on Puget Sound as of this writing, bearing no resemblance whatever to the turbo-electric ferry she once was.

The Key Route plodded along until the Bay Bridge trains took over on January 15, 1939, then held their fleet in reduced operational status until the World's Fair opened on Treasure Island in the spring of the same year.

In addition to their three remaining boats, the Key Route had purchased the *San Pedro* from the Santa Fe and renamed her the *Treasure Island,* in addition to leasing the *Sierra Nevada,* the *Oakland,* and the *Piedmont* from the Southern Pacific. At first, a ferry was operated from both the Oakland terminal and the Ferry Building direct to the fair, and, on holidays and special-event days, additional boats had to be rented to handle the crowds. Both the Fair and the ferry service were operated again in 1940 but they tied up the boats for good when the fair closed at the end of 1940. However, along came World War II and the War Shipping Administration took over the vessels for awhile, then they turned the *Hayward, San Leandro,* and *Yerba Buena* over to the San Francisco Port of Embarkation to operate between Fort Mason and Camp Stoneman, carrying troops between those two points. The *Hayward* burned out a propulsion motor and was scrapped but the other two vessels still fly the Army flag at this writing. The *Yerba Buena* was briefly known as the *Ernie Pyle,* being named for the late great war correspondent, but her name was changed back to the *Yerba Buena* when an ocean-going vessel was awarded the name of *Ernie Pyle.*

The Key Route ferry has passed from the Bay, the Oakland wharf has been demolished, and the electric trains have been rerouted over the Bridge. But the contribution made by the Key in offering the public the finest in ferryboats will always remain an outstanding factor in the progress of San Francisco, Metropolitan Oakland, and the entire Bay Area.

The Key System ferryboat *Yerba Buena,* second vessel of that name, after years of satisfactory service for the Key, continued to serve the Army Transportation Corps as a ferry between Fort Mason and Camp Stoneman.

Last on the list of lines challenging Southern Pacific's bridge of boats on San Francisco Bay, not chronologically but in standpoint of size, operation, and length of service compared to the lines whose histories have been recorded on the preceding pages, was the Nickel Ferry, so named because of the fare charged. This is not to be confused with the better known Creek Route Ferry operated by the Southern Pacific from San Francisco to the foot of Broadway in Oakland. The popular designation of this line was changed from the "Creek Route" to the "Nickel Ferry" during the depression days of 1930 and thereafter until the abandonment of the line because of the company's practice of carrying foot passengers for five cents the trip.

No, the pioneer Nickel Ferry was inaugurated about 1893 by John L. Davies, who later became mayor of the city of Oakland. The Oakland terminal of the five-cent line was practically next door to S.P.'s Creek Route landing, being at the foot of Franklin Street, just one block away. The San Francisco terminal was located at the foot of Mission Street, again just one block away from the Southern Pacific's facilities.

The first vessel to be placed in service was the single-end screw steamer *Rosalie*, built in Alameda in 1893. She was 136 feet long, with a 27-foot beam and a 10-foot depth. Her two-cylinder compound engines produced an adequate horsepower which unfortunately was never recorded, but with cylinder measurements of 15x34x24, quite enough power was bound to be delivered to the propeller shaft.

Unlike the renegade *Rosalie*, the screw-propeller steamer, the two other ships on the line were stern-wheel ships. The two vessels were named the *Elvira* and the *Frank Silva*. Again, unfortunately, no records are today available describing these ships either mechanically or architecturally. It is probable that they were purchased second hand, but in any event their service on the Nickel Ferry was short lived since the line remained in operation but two short years; competition with the more strongly entrenched Southern Pacific was more than the little line could weather and it permanently suspended operations.

CHAPTER IV

WALKING BEAMS
FOR PADDLE WHEELS

LWAYS A HIGHLIGHT of the ferry trip on San Francisco Bay for lads from nine to ninety — and not a few lassies — was the chance to gaze into the inner sanctum of the ferryboat engineer's operating platform below the lower deck, with its unbelievable maze of cams and levers, dials, and bells. The big telegraph dial, with its glaring "Stop," "Full Speed Ahead," and intermediate commands and the big shiny brass alarm gong were among the more terrifying appurtenances of the ferryboat engine room.

For the casual observer, the engine room held a spell of fascination, while for the habitual commuter whose "very own" seat was on the lower deck, the engine room was literally a shrine. When the last express cart had been towed aboard and the milling crowd had found favorite seats on familiar benches after the last train had disgorged its human contribution to the ferry's load, the engineer, attired in his blue serge uniform, put down the magazine he had borrowed from the newsstand, ducked down the metal stairs into the polished chambers that were the capitol of his domain, and grabbed the glistening bar which had been worn smooth by the hands of generations of ferry engineers before him. Slowly he began to raise and lower the bar, causing the paddles to slowly churn sea-froth against a quivering ferry slip so that the deckhands could unhook the huge hawsers from the sides of the slip. Then suddenly the picture changed as the telegraph's bell clattered madly, the big hand on the annunciator dial swung wildly back and forward, finally coming to rest on "Full Speed Ahead" — then for the engineer it was down bar — up bar — down again — up — down for one last time, and with a clattering of metal the reverse lever was thrown into place, the eccentrics came crashing down onto the now-revolving camshaft and the engineer wiped his hands on a handful of waste, looking up at the admiring audience with a quiet air of pride in a job well done — and while the engineer hooked up his starting bar, the fascinated spectator looked out upon the Bay to find to his surprise that the pier had been cleared several minutes before and the boat was under way.

And as the lower deck was toured there were still other wonderful things to see: through various openings and windows in the fidley casing the passenger could see the mystic world of the engineer at work, the vacuum

M. F. SILVERTHORN PHOTO

The walking beam engine and wooden "A" or gallows frame of the steamer
Ukiah. This remarkable photograph was taken when the *Ukiah* was being
rebuilt into the *Eureka* at Southern Pacific Shipyard.

SOUTHERN PACIFIC PHOTO

Chief Engineer Robert Williams (left) and Assistant Engineer Manuel Silviera
in the engine room of the *Sacramento*. By working the bar, the assistant engineer opens the valve ports by hand and so starts the engine.

pump, the eccentric arms, the big crank, all were churning away to the
cadence of the paddle wheels splashing outside in the paddle boxes on the
sponson area. This was the walking beam engine at work, the engine which
had pioneered steamboating on inland waters, and the engine for which
no substitute has ever been offered for sheer efficiency in driving paddle
wheels.

Only the Key Route's passengers were denied the delights of the engine-
room enchantment available to the paddle-wheeling passengers. True, they
too could gaze down on the engineer's control room but a Key departure
was very mild. The engineer stood before a large control panel, replete
with huge knife-blade switches, illuminated dials, fuses, and a huge central
wheel. When the engine room telegraph clanged its "Full Speed Ahead,"
the engineer slowly turned the wheel a fraction of a turn, to the left if the
boat were in Oakland and to the right if the boat were in San Francisco.
As he turned, the propeller shaft slowly started to turn, over and over,
faster and faster. The engineer carefully watched a large dial located immediately over the control wheel and when the flickering needle simmered
down to a certain point, the boat was under way. It was as simple as that
. . . but just as unspectacular.

A Key Route passenger, however, could observe the walking beam on the hurricane deck of Southern Pacific ferries, something not possible for the passengers on the ship itself because the hurricane deck was always forbidden territory. But the beam of a passenger steamer or of a sister ferry on a parallel run was of great interest and generally drew the attention of passengers on a passing craft.

The engine spaces on a ferryboat covered almost the entire hold area. Only the two collision bulkheads located at either end of the vessel prevented the hold from being one continuous space. At one end was the boiler area, the other the balance of the machinery. In a double-end ferry with beam machinery, the end of the vessel which housed the boilers was the permanent forward end and the engines were contained in the after space. This was a formality only, established by the custom on ocean-going ships of having their boiler spaces forward of the machinery space. The vessels were very flexible and they could operate equally as well in one direction as the other with the exception of those ferries which had their paddlewheels aft of amidships. The further aft the paddle could be located, the more efficient it became. The stern-wheel vessel was ideal as long as the boat was under way, for the wheel was located at the afterpart of the boat and the hull formed a breaker to keep debris and floating objects away from the fragile wheel. But, as previously pointed out, maneuverability of the stern-wheel boat left much to be desired.

The ferryboat boilers were for the most part of the fire-tube type, and all the boilers on the beam engine boats were of this design. The early boiler manufacturers were neither well versed in boiler design nor experienced in boiler construction, and many of the river boats and early ferries were victims of terrible explosions. With some degree of timidity, the proponents of the advancement of steam warily reassembled their damaged hulls, built new boilers, and hoped that a recurrence of the last catastrophe would not have to be endured. With plate of questionable strength, new tie bolts, new stay bolts, the new boiler was placed on the vessel, the safety valve set for a new low in pressures and the once-shaken hull ventured forth on another cruise which might — and sometimes did — result in the "whole kit and kaboodle" being blown heavenward. That, however, was one of the perils to be endured in the pioneer days of the steamboat, too.

The most prevalent boiler of the beam-engined San Francisco Bay ferryboat in its hey-day was the return tube Freeman dryback. This boiler consisted of a huge cylindrical drum with a front furnace, a rear combustion chamber with a multi-layered brick back (hence the name, "dryback"), and fire tubes or flues which returned the products of combustion to the top front of the boiler and hence to the uptakes and stack. Before 1900, all of these boilers were fired by coal, but by the beginning of World War I, coal burners were a rarity on the Bay since oil had taken over almost completely.

The majority of the boats had two such boilers and one vertical or "donkey" boiler for keeping up a head of steam in port when the vessel was not

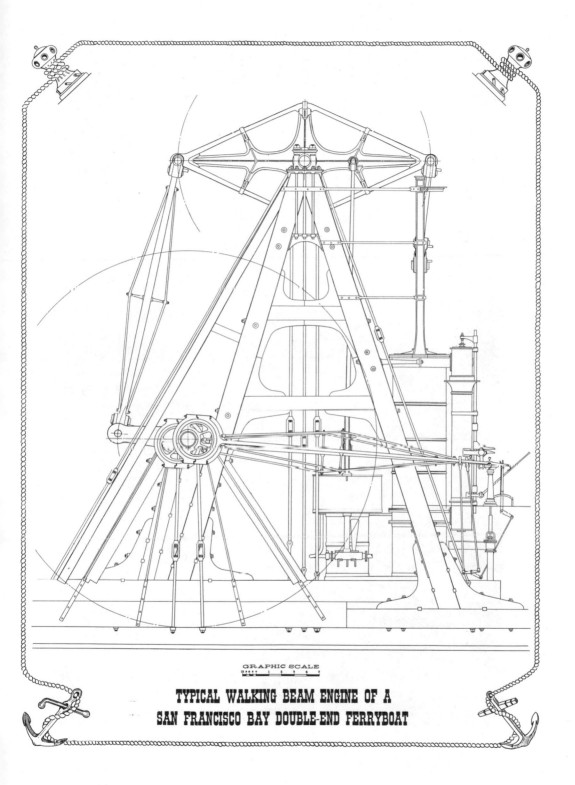

GRAPHIC SCALE

TYPICAL WALKING BEAM ENGINE OF A
SAN FRANCISCO BAY DOUBLE-END FERRYBOAT

Engine face and valve cams of the steamer *Eureka* felt the master's touch as Chief Engineer Edward A. Creighton of the Northwestern Pacific awaited the telegraph signal to start. Creighton's star-studded sleeve shows forty-five years of service on the N.W.P. ferryboats.

in service. The boilers held a tremendous amount of water, took a long time to steam up but an equally long time to cool down. As a result, they held steam pretty well while the boat was tied up at night and took only a brief warming-up period to be put back on the line.

The famous beam engine was the heart of the ferryboat. It took up over five hundred square feet of deck space and extended from keel to hurricane deck. No more sprawling type of engine could have been invented, but this primitive ancestor of our modern steam engines was economical on fuel and maintenance, and it was most effective as a method of driving paddle wheels on its scant 50 or 60 pounds of steam pressure.

Atop the huge engine bed timbers was raised the wooden gallows or "A" frame, at the apex of which was the set of bearings for the beam. On one side was the main cylinder, usually no less than sixty inches in diameter, and having a minimum stroke of piston of eleven feet. An eastern riverboat built in 1854 had a beam engine cylinder of 105 inches in diameter for a fourteen-foot stroke of piston. The monster casting was so tremendous that upon its completion the builders drove a carriage through it and later dined twenty-two persons within the confines of its walls.

Opposite the cylinder was the main crank and bearings, the gap between being bridged by the eccentrics which operated the valve mechanism. The piston rod extended out of the top of the cylinder and was directly connected to the crosshead. Two linkage rods connected the crosshead to the walking beam. The walking beam operated the crank for the paddles through the main rod and also operated the vacuum pump through a long rod attached to a pin closer to the axle of the beam than the pins for the piston and crank ends of the beam.

The majority of the walking beam boats were jet condensing; that is to say, the exhaust steam was mixed with a spray of salt water which produced a vacuum on the exhaust side of the main engine, and this conglomerate of steam condensate and salt water was pumped overboard by the vacuum pump. Some vessels were equipped with surface condensers of the shell and tube type, where the exhaust steam vapors were cooled on tubes through which sea water was circulated and the condensate was then pumped by the vacuum pump into a "hot-well" where it was refed back into the boilers.

The Central Pacific ferry steamer, the *Piedmont*, was the only beamless beam engine type vessel on San Francisco Bay, but it deserves special mention here. The cylinder was inclined from hold level toward the crank and was directly connected to the crank, missing all the trappings of the beam and its accessories. With a cylinder diameter of 57 inches and a stroke of fourteen feet, the vessel's engine was operated in similar fashion to the conventional beam engine. The pride of Chief Engineer James Wosser, who spent most of his working days on the *Piedmont*, the engine was unique on both the Bay and tributary rivers.

About the year 1920, the wooden "A" frame disappeared from the Bay and all vessels not converted to a steel-framed structure were soon out of

Fireman Victor Legaras stands alongside the walking beam of the *Eureka* and is dwarfed by contrast to the giant web of steel.

service. The survivors were all equipped with the more substantial steel framework. The wooden frames were a remarkable piece of construction, with their huge through bolts, tie rods, and stabilizing wooden knees. Although made of hardwood of the finest grain, the working of the engine soon resulted in a general loosening of the frame, and when centers could no longer be maintained while the engine was in motion, it was either rebuild or turn to steel construction. The steel frames were not in the majority on the Bay, however, only the *Oakland, Sacramento, Eureka,* and *Cazadero* being so equipped. When mentioning the typical beam engine of San Francisco Bay, it should always be considered as having a wooden gallows.

The beam itself was a cast steel unit, strapped with a forged steel rim which was keyed onto the spokes. Most of the connections of the major working portions of the engine were keyed in place with "U" straps and taper keys driven home with hammers. The primitive design prevailed until the end. The beams were from twenty to twenty-four feet between the centers of the extreme bearings and a man standing alongside for comparison would certainly be dwarfed.

In the engine room on the operating platform were the four valve stems for the single cylinder, two for exhaust and two for live steam. These stems were operated by cams driven by the eccentrics or by hand as desired. The single-end boats had automatic valve motion in the forward direction only, having to be hand-operated while backing. At the top of the valve stem guides were the three engine room instruments: On the left was the vacuum gauge, in the center the engine room clock, and on the right-hand side was the steam gauge. Polished plates below usually designated the vessel's name and her ownership.

Unusual as they were, the beam engines did not monopolize the powering of ferry boats on San Francisco Bay, it is true; there were compound engines driving paddles, double compound engines driving propellers, triple expansion engines driving propellers, and electric motors driving propellers. But looking back on the early days, the beam engine was the pioneer, the engine which propelled the historical vessels which established regular service on the ferry lanes of San Francisco Bay.

From a performance study of the various types of propulsion used on ferryboats, the conclusion was reached that the initial cost of installing the walking beam engine was less than the cost of installing any other type; moreover, the walking beam engine consumed less fuel than any other type of propulsion with the exception of the diesel-electric adaptations, but in this case the diesel burned a fuel which was of a higher refinement than that burned by the boilers in a beam boat and hence was more costly. It is unusual that such an ancient form of propulsion was able to stand up so favorably against the modern types.

Yes, some readers may simply browse through this chapter, not being too interested in finding out "what made the ferries tick," others will find it of interest because of the explanation of the mechanical details, but no true lover of the ferries who remembers the ever-new departure of the boat on each trip will find anything herein except a wonderful recounting of things that were once taken simply for granted and, now gone, are wondrous memories to recall.

Chapter V

PETER DONAHUE'S MAIN LINE

IONEER of the North Bay ferry lines was Charles Minturn, the man who had been so methodically eliminated from the East Bay ferry traffic in 1866. Minturn recognized his opposition at an early date and turned to a new field before he lost his economic fight in the old one. He obtained approval from the California Legislature on April 18, 1862, to construct a railroad from Petaluma to Haystack Landing and, when built, was operated in conjunction with the two Minturn ferry steamers, the *Clinton* and the *Contra Costa,* until the aggressive ferryman's demise. The line was opened for traffic in July, 1864, and enjoyed a short period of prosperity but, as formerly, the Minturn hard luck dogged the owner and competition from a more powerful rival company forced his administrator to sell the properties to the syndicate which later became the North Pacific Coast Railroad. The ferries were leased by the Contra Costa Steam Navigation Company to the newly-formed San Rafael & San Quentin Railroad, the fortunes of which will be detailed later in this chapter.

It is with Minturn's final adversary that we now concern ourselves and, to realize the importance of this man, some of his earlier exploits prior to his entrance into the marine traffic industry on San Francisco Bay will first be detailed. Peter Donahue, machinist, molder, millwright, naval architect, marine engineer, gold miner, stamp mill operator and designer, executive, financier, railroad builder, steamboat operator, and a worker in a hundred other enterprises, was one of the most brilliant men in early San Francisco. To tell of what Donahue *didn't* achieve would take less space to tell than what he *did.* Today, at the corner of Bush, Battery, and Market Streets in San Francisco, stands the monument erected to his memory, the work of the brilliant sculptor, Douglas Tilden. Mr. Tilden molded representations of the various crafts on the monument, but they are figurative only, for if the works of Donahue were depicted in a single monument, it would needs be of gigantic proportions, dwarfing the masterpiece of Tilden's.

Peter Donahue was born of Irish parents in Glasgow, Scotland, on January 11, 1822. As was the custom of that era, he was put to work in a factory at the age of nine and had been working for four years when his parents came to America in 1835. The Donahues settled in Matteawan, New York, where Peter continued to serve in a factory for the next two years, and then turned to farm work to round out his continuous education. The family then moved to Paterson, New Jersey, and this move can be considered the real turning point in Peter Donahue's career for he embarked on a life in new fields, formed everlasting friendships, and started on his brilliant and rapid rise to fame and fortune.

Peter and his two brothers were indentured, or "apprenticed out," to Thomas Rogers, locomotive builder, Peter as a machinist, James as a boiler maker, and Michael as a molder. Later, Peter was also permitted to learn the millwright trade and also worked for some time in the foundry. He became a master in every trade he undertook to learn, decisively contradicting the old adage, "Jack of all trades, master of none." Tom Rogers had a great and real interest in his versatile apprentice and a firm friendship was formed between the two men which later resulted in Donahue purchasing Rogers-built locomotives for his railroad in far-away California. Peter Donahue was always loyal to his associates and his kindly nature was ever in the fore, even to the point of doing business exclusively, as far as possible, with the friends who had helped him climb the ladder of success. The Donahue empire was founded on friendship and a wholehearted interest in all the enterprises that formed it, two factors of personality that lasted for a lifetime.

Peter Donahue's next adventure was one which shifted his scene of operations and eventually led him to California. He went to work for a firm which built the gunboat *Rimac* for the Peruvian government, the work occupying about two years' time. When the vessel was completed, the Peruvians offered jobs in the engine room of the vessel to the Americans since steam propulsion was new to them. Peter Donahue became assistant engineer and in a short time he found himself bound for Callao, Peru, 'round the Horn. The *Rimac* was the first American ship to steam through the Straits of Magellan, so Peter Donahue was making history already.

Donahue remained in Peru until 1849 when he heard of the discovery of gold in California. He quickly made up his mind to "head for the diggin's" and booked passage on the Pacific Mail Steamship Company's *Oregon*, bound for San Francisco. But one of Donahue's few reverses in his life befell him when he contracted tropical fever on his way and had to be set ashore on the island of Tobago to recover. On the *Oregon's* following northbound voyage Donahue resumed his voyage but this time it was the vessel that broke down. Her engineers threw up their hands since there were engine parts required that appeared impossible to make and the only prospect in view was to make the remainder of the voyage under sail. But the ship's provisions were insufficient to last for what would then be a lengthy voyage. What to do?

The predicament might have been critical had not Peter Donahue been aboard. Passenger Donahue donned his work clothes, surveyed the damage, and inventoried the tools at hand. Yes, he could repair the engines — at least, he could make enough temporary repairs to enable the ship to complete her voyage. Donahue went right to work, the engine plant went back into service, and the *Oregon* steamed on to California with Peter Donahue supervising the operation of all machinery. So elated were the Pacific Mail's engineers when the ship arrived safely in San Francisco that they presented Donahue with one thousand dollars and the offer of a position with the company. Although this was faring quite well for a newcomer, Donahue declined the offer. He had come to California to dig for gold and make his fortune, not to repair engines on disintegrating ships.

But six months in wayward canyons and lawless camps was enough for the future capitalist and benefactor. The heat, the high cost of supplies, and the meager gold yield from fields already worked over by those who had come before him soon dissipated his desire to make a million in mining. He saw the need of many kinds of machinery in California generally and he felt that his trade would bring him riches far greater and quicker than by panning the river bottoms. He went to Sacramento and set up a floating sawmill on a scow for the Phoenix Company, then returned to San Francisco.

During the years which Peter had spent in South America, his brothers James and Michael had not been idle. The two had gone to San Diego, Mexico, during the U.S. - Mexican War and there had maintained an establishment for the repair of ships for the United States Government. James had become superintending engineer of the yard, and at the close of the war he followed Peter to California. The two brothers met in San Francisco in 1850 and promptly went to work to set up the "Union Iron & Brass Foundry" in a tent on Montgomery Street near Jackson. The third brother, arrived in San Francisco later in the year and joined the partnership, the firm moving to more permanent quarters at First and Mission Streets.

The first iron molding produced in California was cast by the Donahue Brothers. The first casting was a part for the engine of the steamer *McKim* and for it the brothers were paid the fabulous sum of one dollar per pound. But parts and material were exceedingly scarce in San Francisco so the figure was not exorbitant. The foundry engaged in various types of work for many different industries, having a number of California "firsts" to their credit. The first printing press in the state, for example, was made by the Donahues and it, in turn, printed the paper which first reported the admission of the state into the Union. The mining men soon showered the foundry with work and, as a result, the brothers built the first quartz mill in California. Michael Donahue retired from the firm in 1857 and moved to Davenport, Iowa, where he became mayor. James assigned his interest to Brother Peter in 1861 due to ill health and died in 1862. Peter then went into partnership with H. J. Booth, himself a master craftsman.

When Peter Donahue came to San Francisco, he was appalled at the absence of gas illumination. He worried about it for the next two years and finally resolved to do something about it. In 1852, he founded the San Francisco Gas Light Company, serving as its president for over twenty years. He obtained a contract from the city to furnish gas for the illumination of the streets and on February 11, 1854, the city's streets were lighted for the first time. The gas light company was highly successful and in thirty years' time it had a capitalization of ten million dollars. In later years after Donahue's death, the company was absorbed by the Pacific Gas and Electric Company.

Although he had always been interested in ships and steamboating, Peter Donahue's career in inland navigation began in 1857 when he commenced to charter and operate river steamers between San Francisco and Sacramento. He was not the first in this field but he engaged quite successfully in river traffic once he became interested in inland navigation. His first vessels lacked the speed of some of his competitors' boats, especially the swift *Antelope,* owned by the Van Pelts. This famous river steamer had carried the first pouch of Pony Express mail from Sacramento to San Francisco on April 15, 1860, and her honor and pride were thus of sufficient importance as not to be trifled with. But Peter Donahue made a challenge with his steamer, the *Sacramento,* which he himself had built, and with which he did beat the *Antelope,* finally forcing her owner-master to transfer her to the Donahue line, where David F. Van Pelt was retained as captain.

The first government vessel to be built on the Pacific Coast was the U.S.S. *Saginaw* and it was Peter Donahue who built her. Her engines were built at the Union Iron & Brass Foundry, and Donahue was not only the builder but the designer as well. She was completed in 1860, the same year in which Donahue built a walking beam engine with a five-foot bore and eleven-foot stroke. For one reason or another, this engine was not immediately placed in service. It was exhibited at the Mechanics Exposition in Union Square in San Francisco during 1864 then stored in a barn for nearly twenty years, after which Donahue used the engine for the power plant in building his first double-end ferry *Tiburon.*

The success of the *Saginaw* gained for Peter Donahue another government contract, this one being let in 1862 for the iron-clad monitor, *Comanche.* Donahue built the machinery, but the plating, armament, and other hull fittings were provided by the government, being shipped around the Horn in the steamer *Aquilla* which arrived in San Francisco Bay on a stormy night in 1863. During the night, the *Aquilla* sank, a mishap which would have discouraged anyone but Peter Donahue. He had never been engaged in salvage in his life, but it was never too late for him to learn. He engaged divers to go down and patch the hull where necessary; he brought in pumps from various yards, and in a matter of hours the *Aquilla* was raised and the material saved. Barely stopping for breath, Peter Donahue laid the keel of the *Comanche* and in three months had her completed without the loss of a single day.

For his first venture in the railroad field, Donahue provided San Francisco with her first street railway in 1861. The line ran across town from North Beach to South Park via Montgomery Street, service being provided by horse-drawn cars. The following year he became interested in steam railways and purchased stock in a company building a railroad from San Francisco to San Jose. He was elected secretary of the corporation and by

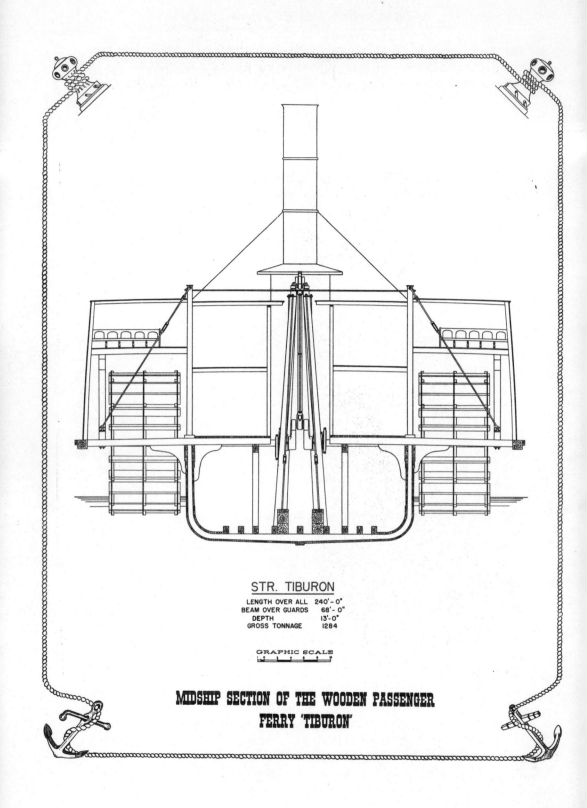

STR. TIBURON

LENGTH OVER ALL 240'- 0"
BEAM OVER GUARDS 68'- 0"
DEPTH 13'- 0"
GROSS TONNAGE 1284

GRAPHIC SCALE

MIDSHIP SECTION OF THE WOODEN PASSENGER
FERRY 'TIBURON'

1863 he had acquired one third of all its capital stock. The new railroad purchased five locomotives from Eastern manufacturers, but it required more motive power and suggestions were made that steam power should be built locally. No locomotives had been built on the Pacific Coast so it was only natural that the first should be constructed by Peter Donahue; besides, no one else was better equipped to do the job. So, in 1865, he constructed two locomotives for the San Francisco & San Jose Railroad and had started two more for the Sacramento Valley Railroad when he sold out his iron and brass foundry to his partner, H. J. Booth. He still retained title to the land the foundry then occupied, near the present-day Third and Townsend Street Station of the Southern Pacific Company, finally disposing of it to Prescott, Scott & Company in 1874. This concern later became known as the Union Iron Works and was finally sold to the Bethlehem Steel Corporation on January 19, 1905.

One of the reasons for Mr. Donahue's sale of his foundry was his widespread interest in the many other enterprises which challenged his imagination and initiative. The same year that he sold the foundry, he had incorporated the Southern Pacific Railroad for the purpose of building an extension to the San Francisco & San Jose Railroad. The line was an important link in the proposed coast route of the Central Pacific and, although Donahue fully expected to be bought out by the larger road, he figured on having as much to sell as possible on the day the sale came. Work progressed southward and Gilroy was reached in 1868. By this time, the "Big Four" of the Central Pacific commenced to negotiate for the line and the sale was consummated on November 4, 1870, for $3,250,000. Peter Donahue made a profit of a million dollars in the transaction and might have been looking around for new worlds to conquer had he not already laid his claim toward some of them.

Flourishing to the north of San Francisco Bay lay the stands of redwood timber, beyond the reach of the railroads and entirely out of the domain served by rail. The San Francisco & Humboldt Bay Railroad Company had served notice of its intention to traverse the north coast with a narrow-gauge line, later realized in part as the North Pacific Coast Railroad. But the interior towns of Petaluma, Santa Rosa, Healdsburg, and Cloverdale presented an easier approach to a land of much promise, and it was there that Peter Donahue struck out. He purchased the franchise of the Sonoma County Railroad Company, which existed on paper only, and by deed of sale dated November 17, 1869, its rights were conveyed to Peter Donahue's standard-gauge San Francisco & North Pacific Railroad Company, and the dirt began to fly.

Grading crews hit Petaluma, Santa Rosa, and all points in between, and Peter Donahue's Main Line was on its way. The starting point was bleak Donahue Landing, on the right bank of Petaluma Creek where the tules grow best. Just forty miles by water from San Francisco, Donahue built his wharf and station, the Sonoma House which was the only hotel in Donahue, and the roundhouse and shops. A few months' time transformed the uninviting swamp land into the scene of a beehive of activity and, from the starting time of September, 1870, until April of the following year, all operations were speedily carried forth to conclusion. The line was then opened for traffic from Donahue to Healdsburg.

The first locomotive of the San Francisco & North Pacific Railroad was formerly the Number Two of the San Francisco & San Jose line. Mr. Donahue brought her with him when he came to Sonoma County, and in addition to her number, she also bore the name *San Jose*. The next four locomotives built for the line were constructed by Donahue's former partner, H. J. Booth, in accordance with Donahue's policy of giving first business consideration to those with whom he had been pleasantly associated in the past. Since he was already in the steamship business on the Sacramento River, his problem of marine equipment to connect his rail line with San Francisco, across the Golden Gate from Marin County, was as nothing. He merely reassigned the *Antelope* to the run from San Francisco to Donahue Landing. The river veteran had lost some of her early-day swiftness but she still rendered satisfactory service under the command of her veteran skipper, Captain David Van Pelt. She served until the company's new steamer was placed in service, this vessel being the palatial *James M. Donahue,* named for Peter Donahue's only son. The ship was designed and built by William E. Collyer, famous Eastern paddle-boat designer, and the engines were fabricated by the Quintard Iron Works, another Eastern concern. It seems somewhat strange that Peter Donahue did not build his own vessels, but he had become so involved in various other enterprises by the time that the *James M. Donahue* was built in 1875 that he had time for little else.

The new vessel was 227 feet long and could accommodate five hundred passengers. Her jet-condensing engine was of the walking beam type which drove the twenty-eight-foot paddle wheels. The single-ended vessel was very fast, had a gorgeous cabin, and boasted of a grand staircase. Captain Van Pelt became master of the new ship and George Scott was chief engineer.

One of the peculiarities of the *James M. Donahue* was her paddle shaft which was located about four feet above the main deck. This was due to her shallow draft and large paddle wheels. Small boys would pull themselves up onto the shaft while the vessel was under way and, by hugging tightly, get a "scenic ride" as they saw one whole revolution through. This practice was not approved by Colonel Peter Donahue (he had become a colonel on the staff of the major general of the California National Guard) and it was stopped whenever possible. But many a sneak ride was to be had when the deck crew wasn't looking.

In 1872, the San Francisco & North Pacific had been extended to Cloverdale on the north and in 1879 an addition had been built south from Petaluma to San Rafael. By 1884, this addition had been extended to Point Tiburon on Raccoon Straits of San Francisco Bay and the Donahue water route was cut by thirty-four miles. This new extension eliminated the effectiveness of the Petaluma & Haystack line and another intruder, the

SOUTHERN PACIFIC PHOTO

The steamer *Antelope*, swift queen of the river, served the Donahue Line in its early days. Pictured above, this sturdy veteran is shown tied to the slip at Donahue Landing. It was the *Antelope* which carried the first pouch of Pony Express mail from Sacramento to San Francisco on April 15, 1860.

Pride of the Donahue boats was the *James M. Donahue*, a single-ended vessel of great speed in her prime. She was capable of 18 knots as her big paddles churned away, and her golden eagle crowned her lofty pilot house.

Sonoma Valley Prismoidal Railway Company. The latter transportation system deprived Peter Donahue of at least one "first." It was the first monorail, or railway using one rail only, in California. The company, incorporated in 1875, proved to be uneconomical and impractical, so perhaps it was just as well that no Donahue was connected with it. The prismoidal line would have ruined anybody's success story.

When the S.F.&N.P. "moved" to Tiburon, the move was truly a literal one. The engine house, the Sonoma House Hotel, the depot, and various other establishments were floated down on barges or carried down on flatcars in one of the largest wholesale moves in California history. Nothing was left at Donahue Landing save the track and wharf and the community, built by the railroad as a long-range development, was deserted by the railroad in a stroke swifter than the one which had occasioned its building. It has been most confusing for historians, in identifying old photographs, to determine which were taken at Donahue or Tiburon in the early days, so completely and exactly was Donahue duplicated on the shores of Raccoon Straits.

With the new trackage came the commencement of commuter service between San Rafael and San Francisco, and for this new service Peter Donahue built his fine steamer, the *Tiburon,* in 1884. Designed by P. Tiernan and built in San Francisco, the double-end ferry was powered by a vertical beam engine built by Peter Donahue himself back in 1860 at his Union Iron & Brass Foundry. As previously stated, Donahue had stored the monstrous engine in a barn and had produced it when it was needed for his new boat. The *Tiburon,* 240 feet long and of 1,284 gross tons, was commanded by Captain Howard White and her chief engineer was Joseph J. Wosser. She was endowed with considerable speed and was frequently raced by her crew against the North Pacific Coast's *San Rafael,* which plied between Sausalito and San Francisco on a parallel rival commuter run. The two vessels were somewhat of a match for speed, a very slight edge going to the *San Rafael.* For part of the journey, the rivals could not even see each other, but as the *San Rafael* left the slip in Sausalito, the *Tiburon* would be sighted nosing around the point of Belvedere Island, black smoke pouring from her "jam-factory" smokestack in an air of defiant challenge. Captain White often resorted to "tactical maneuvers" to gain an advantage in the race, some of these antics dangerously approaching the point of turning steamboat inspectors' hair a pure white, all the while they tried to assure themselves that the rivals were not really racing at all. The engineers joined in the spirit of the occasion by giving the piston a little prodding with the hand bar, and there were crossings made on the Bay whose logs showed no time wasted on the trip. The railroad companies themselves frowned on racing as being dangerous and instructed their captains not to participate in the sport, warning them that demerits would be meted out to any skipper caught racing. And the North Pacific Coast further bluntly stated that not only would demerits be given for racing but that any captain caught losing to a boat on the Donahue Line would be fined double!

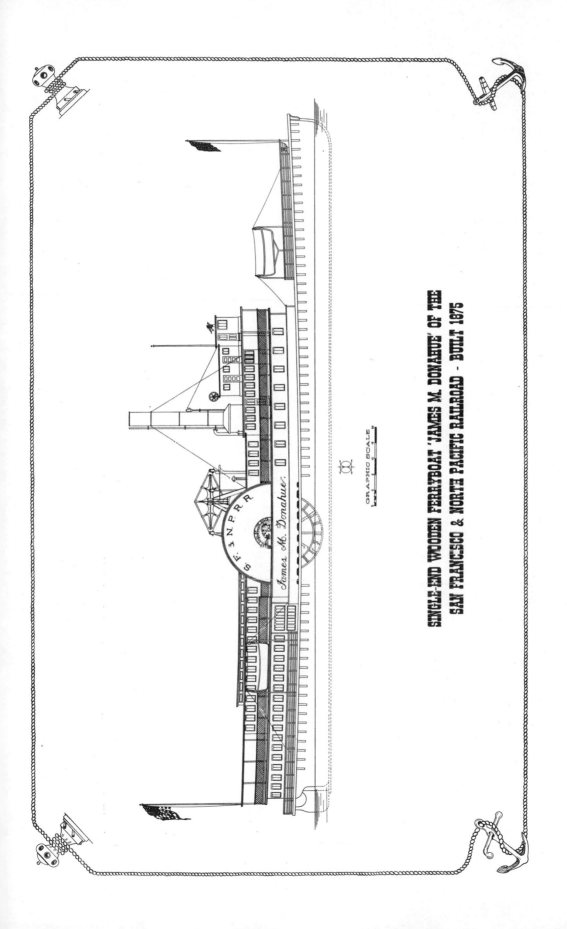

GRAPHIC SCALE

SINGLE-END WOODEN FERRYBOAT "JAMES M. DONAHUE" OF THE
SAN FRANCISCO & NORTH PACIFIC RAILROAD - BUILT 1875

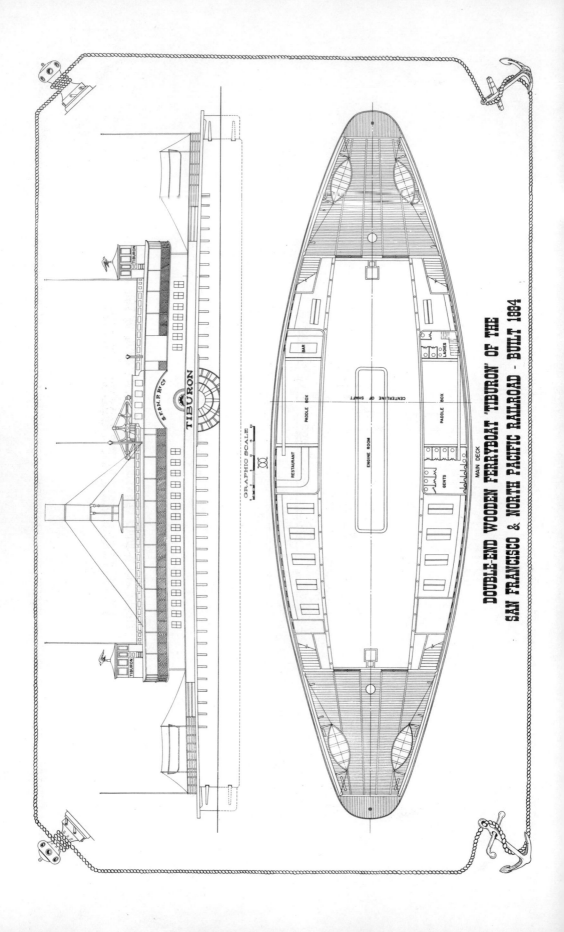

GRAPHIC SCALE

TIBURON

TIBURON

TIBURON

S.F.&N.P.R.Co.

RESTAURANT

BAR

PADDLE BOX

ENGINE ROOM

CENTERLINE OF SHAFT

GENTS

LADIES

PADDLE BOX

MAIN DECK

**DOUBLE-END WOODEN FERRYBOAT "TIBURON" OF THE
SAN FRANCISCO & NORTH PACIFIC RAILROAD - BUILT 1884**

The *Tiburon,* black smoke pouring from her stack in an air of defiant challenge, raced the *San Rafael* for supremacy of the Bay back in the glittering Nineties.

In 1884, Peter Donahue ordered two locomotives for his line, the Numbers 12 and 13. The contract was given to his old friend, Thomas Rogers, of Paterson, New Jersey, with whom he had been employed as an apprentice as a lad. When Peter Donahue made up his mind to purchase the engines, no price quoted by Rogers could have dissuaded him from purchasing them from the man who had given him his start. It was the typical spirit of friendship manifested by Peter Donahue throughout his life; as a demonstration of this friendship, Rogers suggested that they name the two locomotives after themselves. The Number 12 was named the *Peter Donahue* and the Number 13 was the *Tom Rogers.* Unfortunately, this transaction was one of Peter Donahue's last for, soon after the delivery of the two sleek eight-wheeler locomotives, he suffered a sick spell caught a heavy cold from which he never recovered, and passed away on November 26, 1885.

The presidency of the S.F.&N.P. was next vested in Donahue's son, James Mervyn, who outlived his father by less than five years but during whose regime the railroad was extended to Ukiah. With the word Ukiah on the tip of every S.F.&N.P. tongue, it was only suitable that the company's new combined passenger ferry and car float should be named for the new northern terminus of the line. This vessel was designed by the same naval architect who had designed the *Tiburon,* P. Tiernan, and the 291-foot ship was built on the company's property at Tiburon. Such a practice would have warmed the heart of Peter Donahue. The engine was built by the Fulton Iron Works of San Francisco and was of the vertical beam type, originally jet condensing but later fitted with a surface condenser. The *Ukiah* had a capacity of ten standard-gauge freight cars. The vessel was registered at 2,564 gross tons and was used a great deal for picnic excursions on the Bay.

Favorite picnic grounds were located at Paradise Cove and El Campo on the Marin shore, and on Sundays the holiday throngs would line the *Ukiah's* decks to capacity. It has been said that the second mate, after casting off at the start of one of these picnic excursions, would commence his arduous duty of fighting his way through the crowd to the foredeck, to arrive there only in time to make the landing after a forty-five minute trip, so great was the horde of celebrants on a chartered picnic run. The first captain of the *Ukiah* was the faithful David F. Van Pelt and George Scott was chief engineer, both men coming over from the *James M. Donahue*. It may be rightfully assumed that ferrymen live nearly forever, for many of the old-time captains and engineers outlived the steamers under their command. As long as the San Francisco & North Pacific Railroad ran vessels on San Francisco Bay, the team of Van Pelt and Scott were in command somewhere in the fleet.

Shortly after the demise of Peter Donahue, the luck of the racing captains ran out for, on January 14, 1886, the *San Rafael* and the *Tiburon*, San Francisco bound on their 4:30 p.m. trip, collided with each other while

Shown on drydock at the Southern Pacific Shipyard just before she was broken up to become the *Eureka*, the Northwestern Pacific car ferry *Ukiah* undergoes inspection on the marine railway in 1920.

approaching their respective landings at about a 27-degree angle. Both steamers backed off and successfully docked on a second try. The *San Rafael* came off the worse for the accident, her front railing, flagstaffs, lifeboats and other gear were smashed somewhat severely while the *Tiburon* escaped with a broken window.

An honor and distinction accorded the Donahue Company was that of being the first tenant in the new Ferry Building which had been erected to replace the Central Pacific terminal of 1875. The old structure had been progressively torn down as the new building took shape, with temporary arrangements for docking the ferries being made at other locations. On June 15, 1898, the S.F.&N.P. moved in to start the second great era of ferry-boating on San Francisco Bay. The new building, with its impressive tower, became the transcontinental hub of the twentieth century city.

Before this big event, however, the company suffered the loss of the *Tiburon* when she burned in the slip at the old ferry building on New Year's Day, 1893. Most of the upper cabin was destroyed by fire and the photographs and drawings of the vessel as illustrated in this volume depict the boat as she appeared following her reconstruction as a result of this fire. It is recorded that while the underwriters were viewing the *Tiburon's* smoldering remains, the unfortunate watch engineer was questioned as to how much water was in her hold. He inspected the soupy, murky, oil-smeared water in the dank hulk, pondered a minute as though making some mental calculations — then dove in, fully clothed. He reappeared shortly thereafter to contribute the sage report that the water was "over his head."

In the San Francisco & North Pacific Railroad family was an enterprising master mechanic by the name of John Bonner. Bonner was the inventor of all the steering engines on the Donahue boats, the device consisting of a double steam cylinder with a single continuous piston rod and a single piston, steam being admitted at each end of the cylinder through valve ports controlled from pilot house by linkage rods. The extremities of the continuous piston rod were connected to the rudder chains directly, and in this manner the steam cylinder controlled the rudder positioning. Two disadvantages were present in this steering method: The remoteness of the controls resulted in a slow rudder response, and the lack of any locking device prevented the helmsman from holding the rudder in any one position as a flexible approximate position was the only one which could be maintained. This made steering a straight course a virtual impossibility. But the Bonner method was quite satisfactory for ferry use and was certainly an improvement over steering by hand as had been the custom on the earlier ferry vessels.

With the deaths of the Donahues, the moving spirit behind the San Francisco & North Pacific had passed from the picture and new faces came onto the scene to rejuvenate the now rather disorganized system. Headed by A. W. Foster, prominent in business circles in Sonoma County, the California Northwestern Railway Company appeared on the scene. This newly formed group, incorporated on March 17, 1898, leased all the current properties of the S.F.&N.P., on September 20, 1898, and operated them in the name of the newly-formed corporation. By 1902, the California North-western had extended the railroad to Willits and a further extension to Sherwood in virgin redwood country was completed in 1904. In 1907, the Donahue road had been merged with its narrow-gauge rival, the North Pacific Coast, which was then termed the North Shore Railroad and these, together with their subsidiary companies and the existing railroads in Hum-boldt County, were all joined together to form the Northwestern Pacific Railroad Company. The corporate structure of the new railroad system was extremely complex and no attempt will be made herein to analyze its com-position, but it might be of interest to note that both the Santa Fe and the Southern Pacific, through ownership and/or control of various of the subsidiary lines which went into the eventual Northwestern Pacific, retained control after the merger which resulted in the new system.

However, the added floating equipment and ferry history will of course be of interest to the reader as well as a sketch of the narrow-gauge railroad's activity and that of some of its predecessors inasmuch as they became an integral part of the picture of walking beams on San Francisco Bay.

In the 1830's Captain William A. Richardson was granted a tract of land termed the Rancho Sausalito on the southernmost peninsula of the Marin County shore. Richardson remained in contact with San Francisco by oper-ating a sailboat between the two localities, but his operation could never be classed as a commercial ferry venture. For the honor of being the first in this field went to the Sausalito Land & Ferry Company which was formed for the purpose of selling residential lots to persons seeking "a quiet, rural home in a lovely place." As the properties of the land company were of little value to the purchasers without transportation to San Francisco, part of the enterprise, and no small part, either, was the operation of a ferry. With the purchase of a lot, the new landowner got a pass on the ferry, all other travelers having to pay a fare.

The company was rather slow in attending to the details of incorporation and the properties, including the ferryboat, were held in trusteeship by the promoters, prior to incorporation. It is to be regretted that this arrange-ment prevailed since no record of the purchase or origin of the company's first boat, the *Princess,* is available other than that the vessel was probably built in 1859. The Sausalito Land & Ferry Company laid out the streets of Sausalito, naming many of them for the directors of the company, but the street which led to the ferry wharf was called Princess Street in honor of the little sidewheel steamer. The San Francisco terminal for the Land & Ferry Company was famous Meiggs Wharf at the foot of Powell Street, for which a monthly dockage charge of $75.00 was paid by the *Princess's* owners.

The initial trip of the *Princess* was made on May 10, 1868, the vessel being under the command of Captain James Brooks with Thomas Wosser as chief engineer. Thomas Wosser was the first of three generations of Wossers who served in the engine rooms of San Francisco Bay ferries. Superintendent of the company was Captain Charles H. Harrison who had charge of the operation of the ferry. At first, five trips a day were made with the little single-end *Princess,* but on June 28, 1870, the number of week-day trips was reduced by the board of directors to three or four trips daily on week days. Each trip cost $6.00 for fuel besides wear and tear on the boat and machinery.

The Land & Ferry Company was finally incorporated on October 4, 1869, but title to the steamer *Princess* was not transferred to the company's name on the Custom House records until June 19, 1870. Added to the company's marine roster was the slim yacht *Diana* for which the company paid $6,000. She was used for excursions and substituted for the *Princess* when the latter vessel was undergoing repairs or was otherwise out of service. The Sausalito Land & Ferry Company went after their duty of operating the ferry with grim determination as revealed by the company's minutes of the directors' meeting of February 6, 1874, wherein it is stated that "No trip advertised of the ferry shall be omitted under any circumstances except in case of accident or weather. The secretary is instructed to forward a copy of the resolution to the captain of the vessel."

When the railroad finally appeared on the scene, the Land & Ferry Company was not only undisturbed about a successor but eagerly welcomed the opportunity to shift the ferry burden to another concern, and even went so far as to subscribe to $25,000 worth of stock in the new enterprise. The North Pacific Coast narrow gauge took over the ferry operation in 1875, although none of the steamers of the Land & Ferry Company were transferred to the successor or operated by it. The eventual disposition of the *Diana* is unknown, while it has been stated that the *Princess* was broken up around 1881.

Ferry service to San Rafael began with the standard-gauge San Rafael & San Quentin Railroad which was chartered on February 25, 1869, to operate rail service from San Rafael to Point San Quentin with continuing ferry service to San Francisco. The inaugural trip on this road was made March 21, 1870, and for five years thereafter this small line continued to operate, leasing the *Clinton* and the *Contra Costa* from Charles Minturn, the Bay's inveterate steamboat operator. At the time Minturn was engaged in another losing battle, this time with Peter Donahue, as the latter's San Francisco & North Pacific was effectively eliminating his Petaluma & Haystack line. Minturn had acquired another relic of question, the single-end *Petaluma* built in 1857, and he eventually succeeded in palming her off on the San Rafael & San Quentin R.R. along with his other two veterans. Not only was Minturn plagued with hard luck but so were his steamers and the San Rafael & San Quentin glady gave up their struggle when the North Pacific Coast, successors to the Sausalito Land & Ferry Company's ferry business, stepped in and absorbed the standard-gauge line on the promise of operating three trips daily to San Francisco via Point San Quentin.

While it is hoped that it is not really necessary to do so, it might be well at this point to explain to readers who are not familiar with corporate his-

The single-end *Tamalpais*, formerly the *Petaluma of Saucelito*, races the river
steamer *Mary Garrett* down the waterfront of San Francisco in 1888.

tory reporting that it is necessary to backtrack when one course of the company's history has been completed. Eventually the second course runs into
the first, and then it is necessary to go back and pick up another thread to
run out. For that reason, Minturn turns up again and again, while Peter
Donahue reappears on the ferry scene again and again, whenever their activities crossed over the parallel points of history of each enterprise concerned.

The North Pacific Coast Railroad was the outgrowth of a more pretentious corporate title, the San Francisco & Humbolt Bay Railroad Company,
incorporated in 1869. Two years later, abandoning the glowing title and
settling down to an operating name more commensurate with the pocket-
books of the investors, the new corporation was formed December 16, 1871.
The articles of incorporation have been lost during the intervening years
so it is impossible to ascertain all the names of the incorporators, but
among them were Milton S. Latham, one-time governor of the state; James
B. Stetson, of the pioneer wholesale hardware firm; and William T. Cole-
man, the "Lion of the Vigilantes."

Rail exploits of the narrow-gauge line included the building of a single-
track route from Sausalito to Duncan's Mills, completion of which was
accomplished in 1876, and ten years later the track was extended to Cazadero. From San Anselmo (then known as Junction) a line was built to
San Rafael from which point the standard-gauge San Rafael & San Quentin
was converted to narrow gauge on to Point San Quentin. The results of
this rail building were that the North Pacific Coast had a ferry line from

San Francisco to Point San Quentin, an intercommunity rail service from Point San Quentin to Sausalito, and another ferry line from Sausalito to San Francisco. To celebrate the opening of the Sausalito service on the narrow gauge, the railroad company had completely refitted the elegant steamer, *Petaluma of Saucelito.* This was Minturn's former vessel with a new coat of paint and a new method of spelling "Sausalito," an erroneous one which had crept into the records for several years until later corrected.

The *Petaluma* was rechristened *Tamalpais* in 1883 and was the first vessel of that name. Her two Corliss-type engines drove the single-ender's independently operated paddle wheels, and this machinery was the pride of the vessel's chief engineer, Thomas Wosser, formerly of the steamer *Princess.* It has been reported that in the rear of Tom Wosser's engine room on the *Petaluma* there was a lunch counter presided over by one Constantine, surname unknown, one of the classic race closely associated with the restaurant business. The engine on the other side was supervised by Joe Wosser, one of Tom's sons, and in the rear of that room was a bar. Now that the railroad had assumed control, old-time practices of the Land & Ferry days were abandoned for the boats operated on strict schedules, and no longer would the ferry captain hold the departure of his ferry at the sight of a figure flying down the hillside on the run. As for the decrepit *Tamalpais,* the schedule was difficult enough without the added handicap of waiting for passengers.

The ferryboats which came to the North Pacific Coast as a result of purchases of corporations owning them were, on the whole, quite inadequate for the service required of them. This became more apparent as the railroad placed a few months of service behind it, and to relieve the situation two new boats were ordered from an Eastern builder. The two palatial steamers were single-enders equipped with walking beam engines built by the North River Iron Works of New York City. As was then the custom, the vessels were assembled in sections, loaded on the deck of a sea-going ship and transported 'round the Horn to San Francisco. The first of these two identical ferries was the *San Rafael,* completed in 1877. Her sister, the *Saucelito,* built in 1878, enjoyed a much shorter existence than the *San Rafael,* although both vessels came to abrupt endings.

The two ships were masterfully built, considerable thought having been given to both interior and exterior design. Elegant wood carvings and exquisite paneling graced the interior of the cabin, and each vessel boasted two grand staircases. The seats were covered with bright red plush and joinerwork was executed in the finest of polished hardwoods. The lines were exceedingly graceful and both vessels were equipped with a "hog frame" or overhead truss to insure against sagging at the extremities. This feature of inland vessels was quite common among the shallow river steamers but it was unique with the *Saucelito* and the *San Rafael* among the San Francisco Bay ferries. The paddle boxes of the two vessels were ornately decorated with the Great Seal of the State of California in the center and the radial lines emanated from the seal to the outer edges of the

The *Saucelito,* sister vessel of the *San Rafael,* had but a short life on San Francisco Bay when she was burned at the San Quentin wharf of the North Pacific Coast R.R. in 1883.

The glorious little steamer *San Rafael,* famed in story and legend as a result of her unfortunate sinking while carrying a full load of passengers at the commuter rush hour. Her speed and grace will forever be a part of the lore of the Bay.

box. The hull and superstructure were painted white, with red and blue predominating in the trimming. On the foremast was perched a golden eagle, just ahead of the little circular pilot house. There was a golden eagle on the mainmast, too, but it was generally caked with soot from the smokestack.

Although the schedule called for a half hour crossing, the *San Rafael* could make the trip from Sausalito to San Francisco in seventeen minutes if she had to. It was rumored that the *Saucelito* was the faster of the two boats and could even cut more time off the scheduled run, but no figures are available to prove it.

Shortly after delivery of the two new boats, the first marine casualty in the North Pacific Coast's stormy history took place. In 1881, the *Petaluma* was struck by the *Clinton* near Yellow Bluff, the *Petaluma* cutting the *Clinton* in two. The section containing the engines sank near the scene of the accident, and Chief Engineer Manning was among the victims, going down with his ship. The other section, which remained afloat, was towed to Sausalito but proved to be a hopeless loss and was never rebuilt. This accident was followed by a second disaster in 1883, the casualty befalling the *Saucelito*. This vessel and the *San Rafael* were used on the two routes operated by the railroad, and the *Petaluma* was the spare boat. The *San Rafael* usually ran between Point San Quentin and San Francisco while the *Saucelito* was operated between Sausalito and San Francisco. In 1883, the vessels had traded runs for one reason or another, and the *Saucelito* caught fire while tied to the wharf at Point San Quentin. The flames quickly got out of control and enveloped the *Saucelito*, rendering her a total loss. The wharf also burned to the water's edge, and from that time on, service on the San Francisco - San Quentin route was permanently discontinued by the railroad. This left the North Pacific Coast with only the *San Rafael* and the *Tamalpais*, formerly the *Petaluma*.

During the early years of operation the N.P.C. operated single-end boats exclusively and the Sausalito terminal was so situated as to permit the vessels to execute a quarter circle, land sideways to discharge and load passengers, and then proceed, completing a half circle to enable them to return to San Francisco. But the ferry wharves in San Francisco were conventional slips and the Sausalito ferries had to back out and turn around in order to proceed to Sausalito. On a bay where everyone was "out of step save the North Pacific Coast," that railroad finally adopted the double-end ferry, just as had all the other companies.

In another field the N.P.C. set the trend, however. Instead of building car floats complete with engines, the narrow-gauge used barges and tugs, or at least one tug. This vessel was called the *Tiger* and she was the utility vessel of the railroad. She was driven by paddle wheels, the machinery being the product of a Fulton Iron Works machinist named Dennis Gorman. He became so interested in the *Tiger* and her engines that he abandoned the iron works and took the post as chief engineer aboard the tug, working for the narrow gauge. Besides towing the barges, or car floats as they were termed, the *Tiger* would aid in beaching the ferryboats for a superficial drydocking, pulling them off the mud at high tide to return them to service. It is told that on one occasion, the *Tamalpais* was beached so far up that she would not respond to the *Tiger's* efforts to unseat her. Gorman's engines churned and groaned, but the ferryboat would not budge. So the *Tiger* went back for the *San Rafael* and, in tandem, they towed the *Tamalpais* back to deep water. Paddle-wheel steamers are rather ineffective in towing from a dead stop but once under way they exhibit rather remarkable power. Another service to which the *Tiger* was assigned was the dredging of the ferry slips. The company piledriver would sink a tremendous hoe into the mud at the shore end of the slip, and the *Tiger* would drag the hoe and all the silt collected in its path out into deep water with the aid of a drag line. In short, the tug was invaluable in maintenance work around the narrow-gauge terminal.

By 1887, seven trips daily each way were operated by the North Pacific Coast between San Francisco and Sausalito. Boats left San Francisco at 7:30, 9:20, and 11:00 a.m. and 1:45, 3:25, 4:50 and 6:10 p.m. Departures from Sausalito were scheduled for 6:45, 8:15, 10:00, and 11:45 a.m., and 2:30, 4:05, and 5:30 p.m. The fare was twenty-five cents the round trip and monthly commutation tickets sold for three dollars. It is interesting to note that the last trip from San Francisco was scheduled for 6:10 p.m. When the occasion warranted it, the railroad ran an extra ferry for the "theater crowd" and the company took advantage of this trip to haul freight. Many a silk-skirted lady returned from her enchanted evening with gay companions only to be accompanied by a hundred head of beef steers.

The first double-end ferry to be acquired by the narrow-gauge line was the big *Sausalito*, second boat of that name, which arrived on the scene in 1894. The vessel had been built for the railroad at the Alameda shipyard of John W. Dickie. The boat was 256 feet over all in length and was registered at 1,766 gross tons. The vessel was a combination passenger ferry and freight car ferry, and had narrow-gauge railroad tracks on her main deck. Her vertical beam engine was built at the Fulton Iron Works in San Francisco and had a cylinder 56 inches in diameter with a twelve-foot stroke. The engine drove twenty-six-foot radial paddle wheels at a maximum speed of twenty-four revolutions per minute. The vessel was equipped with the first surface condenser on a North Pacific Coast ferry.

As originally built, the *Sausalito* did not have any open deck forward and aft of the cabin at the cabin deck level. Such construction was typical at the time, but two years after she was built, this extended open deck was added, and this feature not only provided additional open-air deck and seating space but permitted the use of a landing gangplank from the side. This enabled passengers to embark and debark from both decks at the same time and materially reduced passenger handling time at peak loads. And peak load on the *Sausalito* was two thousand persons!

Chief Engineer Dennis Gorman of the tug *Tiger* was the first chief engineer of the *Sausalito*. Her first master was a Captain Wilson who was a

Built originally as a combination narrow-gauge car float and passenger ferry, the big steamer *Sausalito* plied the waters of the Bay for 38 years under three companies, the North Pacific Coast R.R., the North Shore R.R., and the Northwestern Pacific R.R. Co.

BETHLEHEM STEEL COMPANY PHOTO

The North Pacific Coast steamer *Tamalpais* leaves the Union Iron Works on her trial trip. Her forty years of service with her original boilers is a record in *Bay* engineering history.

victim of a sad experience early in the career of the ferry. As the boat entered the slip at Sausalito to make the landing, the reverse gear jammed and the *Sausalito* kept right on going. The captain struck each side of the slip trying to break the boat's way, and the dockmaster abandoned his post in a wild dash, meantime yelling, "Look out! She's going to Mill Valley!" The incident so unnerved Captain Wilson that he became unbalanced and was succeeded by John Tribble as captain of the boat.

With the building of the *Sausalito,* the first *Tamalpais* was retired from the North Pacific Coast Railroad. If the company required an extra boat, one was borrowed from the narrow-gauge's cousin, the South Pacific Coast, operating between Alameda and San Francisco. But as the years advanced, even the fleet *San Rafael* had slowed down, and the trouble encountered in backing out of the slip on the busy San Francisco waterfront presented an ever-present hazard. Moreover, the *San Rafael* was too small for the North Pacific Coast service which, by 1895, had increased considerably due to the commuter population which swelled Marin County. So another boat was ordered, the second *Tamalpais.*

Of the first *Tamalpais,* endless stories are told but in her latter days she was a wheezing decrepit oldster on a Bay studded with speed queens. Standing jokes of the time recounted her race with Alcatraz Island, anchored sailing ships, and other stationary objects. Sometimes she was just half there, it was said, with one engine driving one paddle wheel across the Bay in a circuitous, meandering course. Much was expected of the second vessel of that name, for she had been built in 1901 by the Union Iron Works, Peter Donahue's old firm, and this great organization had but recently added a great list of warships to its building achievements.

The second *Tamalpais* was designed by F. B. King and she departed from the walking beam by having a power plant with an inclined marine compound engine driving sixteen-foot radial paddle wheels with feathering buckets. Her double-end Scotch boilers were the latest thing on the Bay and her engine room telegraph, the type with which ocean-going ships were equipped, was new to the ferry field, replacing the "jingle-bells" of an older era.

But the new product gave immediate trouble. Her paddles were too low in the water, she pushed up half the water in the Bay in front of her as she fought her way along the ferry lanes and firing the double-end boilers with coal was killing off the firemen. The Union Iron Works took her back, jacked the engine and the shaft up to the desired level, then added fifteen feet of hull at each end to make a more suitable bow. This solved all the trouble except the hand firing of the coal-consuming boilers. Fortunately for the North Pacific Coast there was a genius in the house. Master Mechanic William J. Thomas had built locomotives in Sausalito, even building the first successful oil-burning, cab-in-front, water-tube-boilered locomotive in the world. Part of Thomas' duties were to attend to the machinery on the floating equipment. Thomas had suggested oil-firing of the boilers long before, but the marine firemen, remembering the *Julia* of

Southern Pacific days and her explosion at Vallejo in 1888, balked at the idea. But the boilers on the *Tamalpais* brought them around to seeing Thomas' point of view, and a month after the vessel was placed in service, the coal bunkers were vacated for all time. No trouble was experienced in burning oil and in achieving proper combustion, and to Thomas' list of successful ventures was added the fact that he was the first person to install successful oil-burning apparatus on a San Francisco Bay ferryboat.

Bill Thomas was a remarkable man, a master mechanic in the days of many great mechanics and of pioneers in the field of steam machinery. On one occasion, the *Sausalito* broke her outboard bearing for the paddle shaft. Thomas surveyed the job, took a few dimensions, and cast another bearing of greater proportions than the first. The new one held up for the life of the vessel. "We had no engineering in those days — we just had to try what we thought was right and hope for the best," he said. But it was Bill Thomas and scores like him who took the first brave steps in the advancement of machine design who paved the way for the more formalized type of engineering of the present day.

On November 30, 1901, the fog settled down heavily on San Francisco Bay. All was dead calm, the sort of eerie stillness which seems to descend when impending tragedy is about to strike. It was ten minutes after six in the evening, and Captain John Taylor MacKenzie looked down from his little round pilot house atop the steamer *San Rafael* and saw the last passenger step safely aboard the deck below. The white-haired old captain, a resident of the city of San Rafael, was the most beloved master in the North Pacific Coast fleet and, indeed, one of the most respected personages on San Francisco Bay. Captain MacKenzie rang down the command to Chief Engineer James Jones to back out of the slip, and the little queen quivered and creaked as the paddles churned away. For the *San Rafael*, it was to be her funeral day — her golden eagles, her gay paddle boxes, her glamour, and her grace — would be further remembered in legend and in prose, but the gallant queen was to run no more.

Captain MacKenzie had made hundreds of crossings in fogs without incident. Visibility was poor, as poor as any he had ever experienced and it was "Slow Bell" almost all of the way. As the ship came abreast of Alcatraz Island, a huge mass loomed up suddenly out of the soupy mist, a mass too big to avoid — too close, too terribly close to the *San Rafael*. It was the N.P.C. steamer bound for San Francisco, also proceeding under "Slow Bell." The *Sausalito*, for it was she, hit the San Rafael a hard blow and Captain Tribble's ship rammed a gaping hole in the smaller boat just aft of the paddle box. The deck crews were alerted and lashed the vessels together temporarily to permit the *San Rafael's* passengers to walk to safety over a plank to the haven of the *Sausalito*. The cook in the restaurant was killed, and two passengers were drowned. Many passengers jumped into the water, but this was really unnecessary since the San Rafael did not sink for fully twenty minutes after the crash.

One passenger, who was in the restaurant at the time of the accident, lost an ear during the melee of the crashing of timbers. Customarily, he was not often seen in the restaurant when on the ferry, usually frequenting the bar on the opposite side of the steamer. He later stated that had he been in the bar "where he belonged, he never would have lost his ear!"

Of all the incidents which occurred during the sinking of the *San Rafael,* the loss of the horse which was kept on board the vessel to haul express carts on and off the steamer was one of the most heart-rending. The animal could not be persuaded to walk across the plank to the *Sausalito* despite the fact that he was given every possible assistance. Like the seamen of old, he went down with his ship, to become forever immortal in the annals of the exploits of the inland sailors of San Francisco.

Captain Tribble was blamed for the accident and lost his position accordingly, Charles Johnson, first officer of the *San Rafael,* replacing him. Captain J. T. MacKenzie became captain of the *Tamalpais.* Dennis Gorman, former chief engineer of the *Sausalito,* became chief engineer on the *Tamalpais* and was replaced on the *Sausalito* by Frank McGuy.

The sinking of the *San Rafael* was the inspiration for Jack London to write his famous story, *The Sea Wolf.* The talk of old-timers for years after, the mishap was vividly revived in memory again in July, 1921, when the steamer *Matsonia* hauled up her anchor — only to find the walking beam of the *San Rafael* impaled on the hook!

With only the *Sausalito* and the *Tamalpais* remaining, the North Pacific Coast was still sadly in need of a boat. The railroad spent considerable money in satisfying judgments handed down in lawsuits brought on behalf of persons who were supposed to have been lost on the *San Rafael.* Shortly after this event, a collision befell the railroad between San Anselmo and Tomales which resulted in more deaths and additional lawsuits. To add to the trouble, the train which ran over the line to retrieve the dead and carry mourners to the funeral was derailed and wrecked on a high trestle, adding injury to injury. Demoralized, the owners of the North Pacific Coast decided to sell their way out of trouble.

In 1902, the transaction was consummated, the purchaser being the North Shore Railroad. At its head was John Martin, the father of long-distance high-voltage electric transmission lines, having built a line of this type from a power house in the Sierra Nevada to San Francisco Bay, a distance of several hundred miles. Associated with him was William Rank, general manager of the East Bay Street car lines, and he became general manager of the North Shore. The object of the new company was to electrify the inter-urban system of the North Pacific Coast from Sausalito to Mill Valley, Fairfax, and San Rafael. To their staff was added A. H. Babcock who later became consulting electrical engineer for all the Harriman lines; F. T. Van Atta, and E. H. Schaubel, who later became top men in the electrical department of the later Northwestern Pacific Railroad; and Paul Lebenbaum, who began as an apprentice with the General Electric Company and who later became chief electrical engineer for the Southern Pacific Company.

One of the first acts of the North Shore Railroad was to tear down the ferry terminal at Sausalito and to build new wharves and a depot. The new arrangement provided both narrow- and standard-gauge track, as the electric equipment was manufactured for standard-gauge operation only. The ferry slips were built for the use of the double-end ferries and provided for embarkation and debarkation from both the main and cabin decks.

Next on the agenda was the procurement of a new ferryboat to replace the *San Rafael*. The contract for her design and construction was let to the Dickie Brothers, boat builders, in Alameda. The vessel was 256 feet long and was registered at 1,682 gross tons. She was named the *Cazadero* after the northern terminus of the narrow-gauge railroad line. The machinery consisted of a vertical beam engine, surface condensing, built by the Risdon Iron Works and which developed 1,600 horsepower. The twenty-six-foot paddle wheels turned at twenty-four revolutions per minute. The boat was launched in the spring of 1903 and on her trial trip on May 19, 1903, she made fourteen knots, a very tidy speed for a ferry steamer.

But initially the *Cazadero* was considered a failure, her early performances not proving up to expectations. Some blamed her poor showing on the fact that she had been built during a shipyard strike and workmanship had accordingly been sacrificed to meet a delivery date. But at least part of the trouble was due to the design, for the stability of the vessel when floating at her deep load line was exceedingly "touchy." The effect of a strong wind against the ship's side or a surge of passengers to one side or the other caused the vessel to "heel" and remain heeled over until some counteracting force righted her, for she had little righting moment of her own.

Built in 1903 for the North Shore Railroad, the *Cazadero* and her hogdeck was a familiar sight on the bay for many years. She was built at the Alameda shipyards of John W. Dickie.

The sternwheel car float *Lagunitas* was originally built for narrow-gauge equipment by the North Shore and converted to standard gauge by the Northwestern Pacific. Her questionable speed often caused her to challenge anchored sailing ships to races which the *Lagunitas* never won!

The fault was partially remedied by adding about 600 tons of railroad iron and cement to her hull in the hold as ballast, but this addition increased her draft and placed the paddles too deep in the water. This cut down the efficiency of the paddle wheels as well as the resulting speed of the vessel, but the company overlooked this trouble since the *Cazadero* was still capable of making the scheduled crossing of thirty minutes. John A. Matheson was the first captain of the *Cazadero* and Frank McGuy was chief engineer.

The North Shore built another boat in 1903 at the Dickie yard, this vessel being the sternwheel carfloat, the *Lagunitas*. The engine for this vessel was built at the Risdon Iron Works, as had been the motive power for the *Cazadero,* but the new engine was a poppet-valve cross-cutoff surface condensing engine. The boat had a capacity of ten narrow-gauge freight cars, but was later converted to carry standard-gauge cars. Harry A. Hyde was her first captain and John Andrews was her first chief engineer. Unfortunately, the *Lagunitas* had a brief career on San Francisco Bay, for her wooden hull was not sheathed with copper plates on the underwater body as was customary for wooden ships. As a result, the planking was soon wasted away due to the action of marine growth and the vessel was dismantled at Sausalito, her hull finally disintegrating on the mudflats in the early Twenties.

After the North Shore completed electrification in 1905, negotiations were begun for consolidation with Peter Donahue's San Francisco & North

Pacific Railroad. As previously stated, the merger came about in 1907 and the Northwestern Pacific Railroad was the resulting corporation. The new company was bristling with floating equipment, for the passenger ferries *James M. Donahue, Tiburon, Sausalito, Tamalpais,* and the *Cazadero,* together with the car floats *Ukiah* and *Lagunitas* were now all sailing under one house flag. Shortly after the merger, passenger service to the Tiburon terminal was discontinued and the standard-gauge steam trains were all operated from the Sausalito terminal. The Tiburon ferry was thus eliminated and only the ferry line from Sausalito to San Francisco was maintained.

A ferry line was established between Sausalito and Tiburon and Belvedere. The *James M. Donahue* was the first ferry assigned to this service, the Northwestern Pacific being rather glad to use this single-end veteran in a service where she would be kept away from the busy Ferry Building in San Francisco. Her backing and other necessary maneuvering when leaving the slip in San Francisco rendered her a helpless sitting duck, literally awaiting a calamity to befall her.

The passenger ferry from Sausalito to Belvedere and Tiburon proved so little productive of business that it became uneconomical to use the *Donahue* in the service, despite the fact that she was the smallest passenger vessel in the Northwestern Pacific's fleet of ferries. The company remained on the lookout for an even smaller vessel, and one was finally discovered which could be altered to fit the bill. She was the tiny steamer *Requa,* built in 1909 in Vancouver, Washington, 97 feet over all and admeasuring 101 gross tons. She was converted in the same year of her building to a passenger ferry and placed on the Sausalito-Tiburon ferry run. She had a tiny boiler and a small triple expansion engine for power, and she ran along like a smooth-running sewing machine. The vessel had a single propeller, although the outline of a paddle box was painted on her hull with the name of the Northwestern Pacific lettered on it. This was in keeping with the general painting scheme of all the ferryboats. James Jones, the former chief engineer of the *San Rafael,* was chief engineer of the *Requa* for both the two short years of her existence. It is to be regretted that this trim little vessel burned to the waterline in 1911, although the hull below that point was saved. The fire was apparently caused by some mishap in connection with the vessel's boiler, so, when the *Requa* was rebuilt, a Standard gasoline engine was substituted for the steam machinery. The superstructure was redesigned and the vessel rechristened the *Marin* and placed in service between Sausalito and Tiburon with a stop being made at the tip of Belvedere Island to pick up and discharge passengers. Victor L. Verdellet was the captain of the *Requa* and also became master of the old-new *Marin.* The little vessel operated on her own private run for thirty years when service on this route was replaced with bus transportation.

The ailing *James M. Donahue* saw little service after she relinquished the Tiburon run in 1909. Her general condition plus her handicap due to being a single-ended boat put her on the beach, to use a nautical expression.

The engineers had become so used to the double-end ferries and the ease of handling the engines on doube-ended craft that they would fake an attack of rheumatism or feign temporary blind staggers before they would take an assignment to the engine room of the *Donahue*.

"Seems like when the Captain rung down to back out of the slip, he'd wait until you backed out fifty miles — and all of it by working that infernal bar by hand," one of her former engineers used to say. It must be remembered that the single-end boats had no way of backing up through automatic valve motion. Every stroke had to be initiated by working the bar.

The *Donahue* lingered around the dolphins at Sausalito and Tiburon until 1921, finally to be towed away to Point San Quentin after her engines had been dismantled. She served as a bait and fish shop, with fishing privileges being extended to cash customers, the privilege of casting their lines into the Bay from the rail of the former queen of Peter Donahue's Main Line. It was a sad and sorry ending for the once-palatial steamer for death was slow and cruel on the soggy, silty shore. . . .

> Ferry Queen, your paddles silenced,
> Your sleek hull has seen its day;
> Most inglorious is your ending —
> On the mud-flats of the Bay.

Next to surrender to advancing age was the *Tiburon,* a vessel of less sturdy construction than the *James M. Donahue.* Although the vessel had been fitted with a Braun surface condenser in 1918, the *Tiburon* required increasing repairs to both hull and machinery, especially in the "A" frame for her walking beam. This frame was, of course, built of wood and was held together with tremendous bolts and eyes and turnbuckles. Working as she had over the years, the frame would move on every turn, barely allowing clearance for the big crank to pass through. Her varying centers often caused the engine to become stuck on center during the maneuvering period, and this was very trying on her personnel. This matter brings the very natural question as to what an engineer must do when a beam engine ferry gets her single cylinder stuck on dead center. To say the very least, the situation is most embarrassing and, since there is no quick remedy, much damage may ensue in the meantime.

When this unfortunate occurrence came to pass, as it did now and again, the solution was not complicated but it took a tremendous amount of manpower. Well remembered is one incident in particular when the first assistant engineer came dashing out of the engine room one fine day and hollered down into the fire room, "Hey! Mike! Joe! Frank!" The three members of the black gang scrambled up the catwalk, leaving the boilers unattended for the next few minutes as one of the huge water-tight doors leading into the paddle-box was opened. Then a prypole, stored along the paddle-box for just such an emergency, was pressed into service. The pole was about twelve inches in diameter, eighteen feet long, and had a tip strapped with steel plate. Using the frame of the open door as a fulcrum, the crew

The steamer *Requa* (above) built for the Sausalito-Belvedere and Tiburon run was destroyed by fire and the hull rebuilt into gasoline powered *Marin* (below).

pried the paddle wheel until the engine passed over center, then all was closed up again and the ferryboat was ready to proceed.

But back to the *Tiburon* and her final windup. Here too was a vessel with a past — the former pride of the San Francisco & North Pacific fleet, a boat which had raced favorably with the *San Rafael* and which was powered with an engine from Peter Donahue's own foundry. Her great days were gone although the one which will probably always be remembered is the day the whistle cord got tangled up in the walking beam and the vessel blew a salute on every stroke. In 1924, she served her last useful service as a clubhouse of strikebreakers at Tiburon during the great railroad strike and was finally broken up for scrap.

The entire fleet of the Donahue road was becoming decrepit, for, during World War I, the *Ukiah* was used to ferry heavy loads of railroad cars across the Bay for the United States Railroad Administration. The strain was too much for the old boat, and the Northwestern Pacific obtained funds from the Government to renovate the sagging hull. They pooled a little money of their own with that obtained from the Government and had the *Ukiah* rebuilt at the Southern Pacific shipyard from which she emerged in 1922 as the passenger steamer *Eureka,* named for the town at the northernmost extremity of the Northwestern Pacific line. She was the largest passenger ferry in the world at the time, being 299½ feet in length and seating 2,300 persons. The beautiful beam-engined steamer was the last of ferries with walking beams and paddle wheels to be built on San Francisco Bay. Captain Victor L. Verdellet was her master and he remained her skipper until the Northwestern Pacific discontinued operating ferries. Her chief engineer was Bert Tuckey who prided himself in the mellow chime of her whistles.

The Northwestern Pacific ably carried on with the new *Eureka, Tamalpais, Sausalito,* and the *Cazadero* for the ten-year period between 1922 and 1932 when the *Sausalito* was partially dismantled and towed to Antioch where she served as a clubhouse. Like the Southern Pacific, the Northwestern Pacific engaged somewhat in the automobile ferry traffic, building three ferries exclusively for this service, something that will be detailed in a later chapter. But the Northwestern Pacific's ferry operation was devoted principally to passenger traffic.

In 1931, work was started on a bridge across the Golden Gate and the physical barrier which had been the reason for the ferries began to slowly disappear. Six years of toil in the swift water of "The Gate" and in the windswept sky above it found the completion of the Golden Gate Bridge coming to pass in May, 1937. For a while, it appeared as though the bridge would affect only the auto ferries and that the passenger ferries which had built up Marin and Sonoma Counties during the previous seventy years would continue their faithful service. But the bridge began to slowly sap the traffic from the ferries and in 1940 application was made to the California Railroad Commission for abandonment. At first, the commission requested that a cost-saving reduced operation be tried for six months but

The trim little *Tamalpais* whistles into the Sausalito pier a few days before the ferry operation ceased. This boat was always a favorite with the passengers.

Largest of all the double-end passenger ferries was the *Eureka*, built in 1922. Carrying 2,300 persons, the vessel carried the burden of the Northwestern Pacific's heavy commuter traffic.

this proved to be of no help — the handwriting was on the wall. Possibly a continuance might have been ordered had not the train equipment and the ferryboats been so old. But the railroad would have been faced with rehabilitating and re-equipping the entire system and practical economics, as well as further safeguarding the stockholders' investment, dictated that this not be attempted.

On February 28, 1941, the curtain was rung down on the Marin ferry operation. The trains still rolled on Peter Donahue's Main Line, but his ferry line had breathed its last. The *Tamalpais* would have been the last boat to make the run had it been operated according to schedule, but, anticipating a large crowd of mourners, Superintendent H. R. Gernreich ordered the *Eureka* to make the trip with the crew of the *Tamalpais*, excepting Captain Verdelet who handled his own ship. A band played the *Ferryboat Serenade,* a popular tune of the day and when the engine room telegraph rang down the "Full Speed Ahead" to depart from San Francisco, Lawrence Wosser, grandson of the first Marin ferry engineer, Thomas Wosser of the old *Princess,* stepped up to the bar to handle the engine. He was first assistant with "Little Andy" Disher, but the canny Scot let Larry handle the steamer for sentimental reasons.

Tears were shed and goodbyes said, and the *Eureka* was made ready for a final run the following day, March 1, with many friends of the railroad as invited guests. Master Mechanic Bill Thomas was on hand, along with six captains and six chief engineers of the company who took turns at the

Fireman Tony Simas (right, looking in doorway) watches First Assistant Engineer Lawrence Wosser on the "down bar" as he takes the Eureka out of the San Francisco slip on the last trip, February 28, 1941. Assistant Chief Engineer Andrew C. Disher stands by.

controls. Chief Engineer Ed Creighton with forty-seven years of service represented the old-timers, with Harry Smith being the runnerup. The last leg of the journey was through historic old Raccoon Straits, scene of many an exciting race, and now on the last run the *Eureka* passed within view of the *Cazadero* and the *Tamalpais* tied up at Tiburon. Shopmen had boarded the vessels and blasted a rousing salute to the *Eureka,* last of the Sausalito ferries, as she passed slowly by.

The *Tamalpais* was scrapped at Moore Dry Dock in 1947, while the *Cazadero* was dismantled in 1942, later rebuilt into a barge, and eventually blown up with two tons of dynamite at Hunter's Point in January, 1949. The *Eureka* was leased to the Southern Pacific by the Northwestern Pacific for operation between San Francisco's Ferry Building and the Oakland Pier, departure point for S.P. transcontinental trains and other service. But only in fancy and in fond recollection rock the walking beams and splash the paddle wheels on Peter Donahue's Main Line.

CHAPTER VI

JEFFERSON
OF MONTICELLO

**Y**ES, GOOD READER, you're still reading *Of Walking Beams And Paddle Wheels,* even though the title of this chapter might lead you to think otherwise. It's true that the Jefferson of our present story didn't write the *Declaration of Independence* nor was he ever President of the United States, but he and his "Monticello" made history in the Far West which had been explored by Lewis and Clark at the behest of the original Jefferson, Squire of Monticello. For Zepheniah Jefferson Hatch was born in 1846 on a farm near Monticello, Sullivan County, in New York State. He migrated west to Portland, Oregon, where he went to work for Jim Hill building the Great Northern Railroad.

Early in Jefferson's career, he became interested in marine operations and ran a small steamer on the Columbia River between Portland and an island in the river with cement as his cargo. On one of his trips, however, the cement got wet, expanded, the vessel swelled up, and sank at the dock, although she was later raised. This turned Z. J. Hatch's mind toward commodities other than cement and, in 1892, he placed an order for the construction of a small passenger steamer which he named the *Monticello* after his birthplace in New York. The vessel was built by E. Sorenson at Ballard, Washington, and completed in July, 1892. One hundred and twenty-six feet long, having a 22-foot beam, and an 8-foot depth, the little vessel was admeasured at 227 gross tons. She had a single boiler and a tiny triple expansion engine. Naturally, her first captain was one Zepheniah Jefferson Hatch.

After some rather unfruitful attempts to place the *Monticello* on a profitable and satisfactory run in the Northwest Territory, Hatch decided to explore the possibilities of operating on San Francisco Bay. In 1895 he sailed his little steamer to San Francisco under her own power but just outside the harbor, the boilers became salted and the argosy of the *Monticello* ended rather ignominiously when it became necessary for the Pacific Mail Company to send a vessel to tow the ailing little steamer into the Bay. Following this service, the Pacific Mail served a libel on the *Monticello* but the skipper was able to pay this off and keep his ship. On August 10, 1895, the *Monticello* was placed on the run between Vallejo and San Francisco under the banner of the Hatch Brothers Steamship Company, for

Under her master, Zepheniah Jefferson Hatch, the little steamer *Monticello* started the ferry service between San Francisco and Vallejo. Built on Puget Sound, operated on the Columbia River, a prize at sea, the veteran saw stormy years in distinguished history.

Z. J. Hatch had been joined by his younger brother, Charles N. Hatch, at the time he came to San Francisco Bay.

When the Hatch brothers commenced operation of their steamer, there was one other company operating direct service from San Francisco to Vallejo. This concern was composed of three brothers, Martin, John, and Joseph Aden, who had built the sternwheel steamer *Sunol* in San Francisco in 1890. This vessel was 135 feet long, had a beam of 27 feet 6 inches, and a depth of 7 feet 10 inches. The stern wheeler was admeasured at 294 gross tons and her engine developed about 120 horsepower. The *Sunol* carried both freight and passengers to San Francisco and made a single round trip each day, the running time being about three and three-quarter hours each way.

The *Monticello* made the same journey in about two hours and the company operated several round trips a day. Business prospered for the Hatch Brothers and they had a second boat built for them, the *General Frisbie*, completed in December, 1900. The new vessel was constructed at the New Whatcomb, Washington, yard of G. G. Whidden & Company. She was 184 feet long, 29.3 feet in breadth, and was registered at 670 gross tons. For many years this vessel was the largest ship in the Vallejo company's fleet. Her main engine was built by the United Engineering Company of San Francisco. The vessel was towed down to San Francisco Bay from the builder's yard and the engines were lowered into the hull at the Howard Street Dock in San Francisco.

With two boats at their command, the Hatch Brothers were able to compete favorably with the *Sunol* and their supremacy would never have been questioned had not the Adens chartered the big sternwheel river steamer, the *H. J. Corcoran,* 210 feet long, 682 gross tons, built in 1898. This vessel had a tremendous paddle wheel and lots of power, and she gave the *Monticello* and the *General Frisbie* a hot race to San Francisco. The Hatch Brothers were naturally disturbed but didn't take the blow lying down. One of Z. J. Hatch's acquaintances was R. R. Spencer of the National Bank of Commerce in Seattle. The bank had foreclosed on a swift little steamer named the *Arrow* which had sleek lines and was as swift as the object for which she was named. The vessel had been built in Portland, Oregon, in February, 1903, and, although she was only 147 feet long, she boasted of a 1,000-horsepower triple-expansion engine that really sent the ship flying through the water.

The Hatch Brothers needed her but didn't have the money to purchase her, so the bank offered to finance the venture providing Spencer could buy into the Hatch Brothers Steamship Company. The brothers had been considering incorporating for some time previous and the need of capital prompted them to hasten the incorporation. So, in 1904, they formed the Monticello Steamship Company, the two principal stockholders being Z. J. and C. N. Hatch with R. R. Spencer purchasing one eighth of the total capitalization of $100,000.

The *Arrow* was placed on the Vallejo run in 1905 and she was able to outrun the *H. J. Corcoran* with ease. The Adens then settled for the less pretentious *Grace Barton,* another river veteran of 195 gross tons. The Aden Brothers then relinquished their steamship business to a fourth brother, R. J. R. Aden, who operated a wood and coal yard in Vallejo. He continued to run the *Sunol* until 1913 when the name of Aden disappeared from the scene of Bay steamboat operation and the *Sunol* was sold to the Leslie Salt Company in 1924 and renamed the *Pyramid.* The *H. J. Corcoran* served for many more years on the Bay for the C & H Sugar Company, having been rechristened the *Crockett.*

In the meantime, the Monticello Steamship Company had co-ordinated their ferry service with the electric trains of the Vallejo, Benicia & Napa Valley Railroad which had opened service on July 4, 1905, and train connection was made with the Monticello steamer *General Frisbie* at the Maine Street Dock in Vallejo. The Hatches were very interested in the electric line and had even considered merging with it several times but nothing more than a working agreement was ever reached. The railway later became known as the San Francisco, Napa Valley & Calistoga Railway Company, but it was generally more popularly referred to as the Napa Valley Line.

In 1905, the Hatch Brothers obtained the services of Sam Sutton as general superintendent and port engineer. Mr. Sutton had charge of the operation of the boats, wharves, and the maintenance shop, coming to the Monticello Company from the White Star Steamship Company. He was born of a Quaker family and had learned the machinist trade at the Roach Ship-

The 180-foot *General Frisbie* was for many years the main boat of the Hatch Brothers steamship operation. Her 1,000-horsepower engine opened the speed era on the Vallejo route.

The twin-stacked *Arrow* caused the incorporation of the Monticello Steamship Company and her speed insured elimination of competition on San Pablo Bay.

MONTICELLO STEAMSHIP COMPANY PHOTO

The Vallejo, Benicia & Napa Valley Railroad reached Vallejo in 1905 and opened connecting service with the Monticello boats on July 4 of that year. The *General Frisbie* was the first boat to make train connections.

ROBERT McFARLAND PHOTO

The paddle steamer *Sehome*, rebuilt into a twin-screw vessel, plied the Vallejo run for many years for the Monticello Company. She was sunk in a collision with the *General Frisbie*.

yard in Chester, Pennsylvania. He came West at the age of 24 and rose rapidly as a port engineer for various steamship companies. He was encouraged to join the Monticello Steamship Company by Z. J. Hatch in consideration of an eighth interest in the Monticello Company. Sutton was the backbone of the company for all the years of its existence and he maintained the fleet of vessels in a most efficient manner for his employers.

In 1909, the company bought the sidewheel steamer *Sehome* which had been built on Puget Sound. She was operated as a paddle steamer for about five years when she was converted to a twin-screw steamer. By this time, the company was operating six round trips daily. The *General Frisbie* and the *Sehome* could carry the greatest loads and hence were used the most. The *Arrow* and the *Monticello* were rapidly becoming too small for the traffic and the ferry line recognized the need of a third vessel of larger size. Since no suitable boats were available, the Monticello line decided to build a steamer to their own specifications and negotiations were entered into with the Union Iron Works of San Francisco to build a boat. The proposed vessel would cost about $320,000 — which was $220,000 more than the total capitalization of the Monticello Steamship Company. But business was slack at the iron works, they needed the work, and the Monticello line needed the ship. The bank loaned the Hatch Brothers the money and the vessel was built in 1910, being launched in May of that year. She was the largest of all the Monticello steamers, being 231 feet long, having a beam of 48 feet and a registered gross tonnage of 2,189. Her main engine was built by the United Engineering Company of San Francisco and was a four-cylinder triple-expansion engine developing 2,600 horsepower. The ferry was christened the *Napa Valley* and was capable of doing the equivalent of 21 miles per hour.

The nucleus of a great organization had been formed and the progressive little Monticello line was solidly backed by the citizenry of Vallejo and the officials of nearby Mare Island Navy Yard. The Hatch Brothers had just barely been able to maintain the line in the black during the years of development and many times it looked as though the company just couldn't pull through. The route from San Francisco to Vallejo was a long one, approximately thirty miles, and the Monticello boats had to travel at breakneck speed — considered in terms of Bay ferry speeds — in order to maintain schedule of one hour and forty-five minutes. This meant heavy maintenance, a constant expense which kept profits down. The line operated numerous concessions aboard the boats, such as the restaurant, bar, shoeshine stand, and barber shop, in order to derive as much revenue as possible. The bar had been a top moneymaker for years until it was closed at the request of the authorities in charge of the Navy Yard. Its profits were often the margin between financial solvency for the company and bankruptcy.

Although the struggle was hard, the Hatch Brothers could never complain that they lacked the backing of faithful patrons and for good reason, too. Whenever possible, of course, the company always tried to sell the tar-

Handiwork of the Union Iron Works was the *Napa Valley,* built in 1910, and the first of the trio of large vessels which carried on the Monticello's trade in the Twenties. She was advertised as doing 21 miles per hour.

iff-rated tickets to the enlisted Navy personnel stationed at Vallejo but if a sailor had spent has last nickel making "whoopee" in the Big City, the company never refused him a ride back to Vallejo. The thought behind this policy was the retaining of the Navy's goodwill because the punishment due the sailor for being AWOL was far greater than what the company theoretically lost in fares. It was for just such policies that Vallejo regarded the Monticello Steamship Company as a community enterprise and supported the Hatch line in all its battles with competitors.

Zepheniah Jefferson Hatch, founder of Monticello, died in 1913, leaving his brother, Charles N. Hatch, in command. The company had become well established by that time and the three sons of Z. J. Hatch were raised and educated to carry on the Monticello empire. William D. Hatch was a ferryboat captain. Tremaine Hatch was an engineer, and C. Ferry Hatch was a lawyer. Old Z. J. had always said that he had three troubles in his life: captains, engineers, and lawsuits. He raised his sons to take care of all three.

In 1914, the ferry line converted the *Sehome* from a paddle steamer to a screw propeller vessel. The conversion was quite some feat, although in the Monticello Company, major jobs such as this one were commonplace. The ferry company had obtained the two main engines out of the destroyer U.S.S. *Rowan* and placed them in the *Sehome.* These two triple expansion units each drove a screw propeller through a reduction gear, this hookup being somewhat unique in the marine field. However, the destroyer engines developed their greatest horsepower at about 300 r.p.m. and had to be geared down to operate the *Sehome's* twin screws at about one third of the engine speed. The gears were somewhat unsuccessful and were quite noisy. They were later replaced by a composition fiber gear, but neither set saw much service. This conversion and installation of new machinery was accomplished by the company's own force under the direction of Sam Sutton. The vessel was returned to service on July 1, 1914, making an operating speed of sixteen knots. Thus, the only paddle steamer of the Monticello Steamship Company was changed to screw drive and no other paddle boats were ever again placed on the Vallejo run.

In 1918, at the behest of the Navy Yard at Mare Island, the Monticello Steamship Company increased its passenger-carrying capacity. The yard was hiring war workers who lived in San Francisco and the Vallejo - San Francisco ferries were crowded. The company had lengthened and sponsoned out the *General Frisbie* in the spring of 1918, the work being accomplished at the yard of Barnes & Tibbetts in Oakland. But the twenty-foot lengthening was but a drop in the bucket compared to the need for additional passenger space on the Vallejo run.

At the same time, the flagship of the Sandy Hook fleet, the twin-screw steamer *Asbury Park* of the Central Railroad of New Jersey, had been idle for two years. The vessel had been built at the Cramp Shipyard in Philadelphia in 1903 and was used in the commuter traffic between New York and the residential sections of the Jersey shore. The speedy *Asbury Park* had quite a reputation as a racer on the East Coast, having beaten several other speed queens while splitting the waves at her top speed of twenty knots. Tremaine Hatch and Sam Sutton were sent to Jersey by the Monticello Company to survey the *Asbury Park* to determine if she could be pressed into the expanded service planned by the company. The two men reported favorably on the ship and she was accordingly purchased by the Monticello interests and made ready for the trip to the Pacific Coast under her own power. Captain Fred Warner, a well-known pilot, was captain of the ship for the voyage and Sam Sutton acted as chief engineer. The vessel had two four-cylinder triple expansion engines and nine boilers, developing 5,900 horsepower. She was a coal burner so her decks were filled with coal stocks, sufficient to make the trip. Even the ornate cabin interiors were filled to capacity with coal and temporary living quarters had to be improvised for the crew of sixty.

The *Asbury Park* left Jersey City on the fifteenth of September, 1918, and proceeded at an average speed of eleven knots on her journey to the Golden Gate. She stopped in Havana, Cuba, to recoal, her initial stocks proving insufficient. After the one-day stopover, the ship proceeded on toward the Panama Canal where several of the boiler firemen deserted the ship, the nine hungry boilers requiring too much coaling. Accordingly Sam Sutton had to replace his crew with any type of individual he could recruit. Although the sea was calm enough, the voyage was thenceforth a rugged one because the crew was boisterous and restless, and Sam Sutton slept with a gun under his pillow every night from then on. In twenty-four days the Jersey queen of the waves steamed in through the Golden Gate and tied up just at noon at the Vallejo dock between Maine and Georgia Streets to be greeted by a resounding blast from everything in the vicinity that had a whistle on it — ferries, steamers, locomotives, factories — and Vallejo was a town full of whistles! Sam Sutton and his crew had done a great job and they were accorded a well-deserved salute.

The *Asbury Park* was a sorry sight when she arrived in Vallejo. Her cabins were full of coal dust and she needed painting and refinishing from stem to stern in the worst way. The throng which met her was impressed, nevertheless, for she was sixty feet longer than the *Napa Valley*, then the largest boat. She spent the next six months in the Barnes & Tibbetts Yard in Oakland and at the Monticello docks in Vallejo undergoing repairs which included the removal of the nine Roberts boilers and the substitution of four larger boilers of Sam Sutton's own design.

Before the new ship could be placed in service, however, the Vallejo line suffered a setback which made the *Asbury Park* needed all the more. On December 14, 1918, the *General Frisbie* collided with the *Sehome* just off Pinole, the two vessels meeting in a dense fog. The Monticello line ran six compass courses between San Francisco and Vallejo, and in a dense fog they relied on compasses and channel markers for their position. The times and places for meeting boats coming in the opposite direction were of course known by past experience and this system of "blind steering" had been completely successful ever since the ferry service was instituted. But on this one night, disaster struck. Each of the ships had come to a stop, for the Pinole meeting had been anticipated; but each boat had been sounding its whistle, the blasts unfortunately sounding off simultaneously, with the result that neither heard the other. The *General Frisbie* got under way again, only to collide with the *Sehome* which was still remaining stationary waiting to locate the *Frisbie*.

The gaping hole which the *General Frisbie* punched in the side of the *Sehome* was awesome and an engineer in the engine room of the latter reported that he could read the name *Frisbie* on her bow as he stood on the operating platform of the *Sehome*. No one was injured, fortunately, but the *Sehome* began to sink. The *Frisbie* held her bow into the hole she had punched, thus preventing the other vessel from sinking too rapidly. By a stroke of rare good fortune, the entire Marine Band from Mare Island was aboard the *General Frisbie* and they immediately struck up with *K-K-K-Katy* and other World War I favorites, thus quieting the passengers while those from the *Sehome* were transferred to the *General Frisbie*. This single fact has been credited with having averted panic on the boats.

Although the *Sehome* was valued at $100,000, she was covered by an insurance policy against loss. On the debit side, however, so far as personalities go, was the fact that Sam Sutton was a passenger on the *General Frisbie* at the time of the collision. Captain Fred Olson of the *Sehome* and Captain Carl C. Sandahl of the *General Frisbie* both had their master's

Pride of the Sandy Hook fleet was the Central Railroad of New Jersey's *Asbury Park*. She had quite a reputation as a racer when the Monticello Company bought her and sailed her from New York to Vallejo via the Panama Canal in 24 days. The vessel is pictured above as she appeared on the east coast and below in service on San Francisco Bay.

licenses suspended for ninety days as a result of the collision, regrettable as the accident was and undoubtedly as unforeseeable. Mistakes, it would seem, occur most frequently whenever the boss is around.

The *Asbury Park* made her debut on San Francisco Bay on October 31, 1919, leaving the Vallejo dock promptly at 6:00 p.m. She made the rigid schedule with ease but her heavy wake broke nearly every mooring in the Mare Island Channel. The Navy sent letters to the Monticello officials requesting that the speed of the flyer be reduced while under way in the channel and the company promptly complied. But the speedster didn't know her own strength and often roared unknowingly down the channel, breaking moorings by the dozen.

The Navy, however, had its own day on November 20, 1919, when the battleship *California* got away from the Yard during its launching and wound up almost in the middle of Georgia Street in Vallejo, taking one of the Monticello Company's docks with her as she went. The Navy got the battleship back to a mooring by the end of the day then took her to the outfitting dock the following morning. In the attempts to position her at the latter installation, however, she nearly got away again to sideswipe the Monticello vessels tied up to their own docks. No harm was done and the Hatch company replaced a dolphin at their pier without complaint figuring, thank Heaven, that they didn't launch battleships every day at the Navy Yard.

The *Napa Valley* and the *Asbury Park* were reconverted in 1922 to carry automobiles and the main deck height was increased to accommodate trucks. Despite these changes, the Monticello Steamship Company was still suffering from an old complaint — they always had two ships of adequate size to handle the traffic but they were always needing three. So once again the Monticello men were on the lookout for a suitable vessel and again they found what they wanted on the East Coast. The vessel was the big steamer *Florida* of the Old Bay Line of Baltimore, Maryland. Built by the Maryland Steel Company at Sparrow's Point in October, 1907, the big vessel was comparable to the *Asbury Park* in size although she was but a single screw ship.

The *Florida* cost the Monticello Company $200,000. Samuel Sutton went back to take possession and sailed the ship from Norfolk, Virginia, to San Francisco in eighteen days, arriving on May 11, 1924. Her main deck was rebuilt to accommodate seventy automobiles, she was completely modernized in every respect, and was rechristened the *Calistoga* on October 9, 1924, with a gala open house being held on the vessel from 7:00 to 10:00 p.m., complete with free ice cream. The Vallejo Municipal Band, led by Director Lovegood, furnished music for the evening and the guest speaker was none other than United States Senator Sam Shortridge who praised the *Calistoga*, denounced LaFollette, and went on to encourage the multitude to vote for Calvin Coolidge for President!

The conversion of the Calistoga was an excellent job and, despite the fact that both the Navy Yard and the Bethlehem Steel Company put in strong bids to handle the work, the entire project was accomplished in the Monticello's maintenance shop under Sam Sutton's direction. Later Mr. Sutton installed a bow rudder on the *Calistoga* to enable her to execute the sharp turn in the Mare Island Channel with more proficiency. This rudder was unique in that a section of the stem and part of the fore peak were cut away and the new rudder fashioned in the shape of the underwater bow section.

Vallejo has always been a town that has loved celebrations and the success of the *Calistoga's* christening spurred the town on to even greater heights. The populace had always been dissatisfied with the name *Asbury Park*, feeling properly that such a name had no local significance, and clamored for a more appropriate title. So the Monticello Steamship Company decided to rechristen the ship the *City of Sacramento* since most of their automobile business was derived from traffic originating at or destined to the State capital. The celebration was planned for weeks, and Miss Lilybelle Scott, who was "Miss Sacramento" of 1925, presided over the festivities, assisted by "Miss Vallejo" and "Miss Santa Rosa." "Miss Sacramento" dashed a bottle of champagne against the hull and as the liquid bubbled down the side of the vessel, the band on the upper deck crashed into the *Star Spangled Banner,* sirens on the *City of Sacramento* and other vessels in the channel blasted away, and the crowd stood with bare heads and cheered as the big steamer's name was officially changed, never again to be known as the *Asbury Park.* All of this took place on October 16, 1925,

From the Old Bay Line of Baltimore came the *Florida* to be rechristened *Calistoga* amid much pomp and ceremony at the Monticello Steamship Company's Vallejo dock. Along with the *Asbury Park* and the *Napa Valley,* she formed the nucleus of the Vallejo fleet.

which was California's Diamond Jubilee Year and it had been a banner year for the Monticello Steamship Company.

In 1926, the company widened the *Napa Valley* in order to carry more automobiles, the company having carried 96,000 cars the previous year. Although basking in financial sunshine, the empire of Monticello founded by Z. Jefferson Hatch realized that its days of greatness were numbered. People were beginning to talk about building bridges all over the Bay. The Hatch Brothers had built a gigantic steamship company from nothing with plenty of hard work — why couldn't corporations already possessed of greater capital build bridges? There was even talk of having the Government build them. So Tremaine and Ferry Hatch, sons of Jefferson Hatch and then heads of the company, sold the Monticello Line to the Golden Gate Ferry Company for $2,000,000. This was in February, 1927, and the new company took over on April 30 of the same year. Samuel Sutton passed away one year later and Charles N. Hatch followed him in 1929. The empire of the Hatch Brothers came to an end and, with it, its staunch principal characters also departed from the scene. The little line of Monticello gained greater community pride than any other ferry line on San Francisco Bay, and its thirty-two-year rise from nothing to a two million dollar concern will be remembered among the greater achievements in the maritime history of California.

*   *   *   *   *   *

The purchaser of the Monticello Line was a storybook concern in its own right. With the fairytale name of the "Golden Gate Ferry," a corporation born of nothing but determination and personal effort only to find a pot of gold at the rainbow's end, this concern was built of the same ingredients of which Jefferson Hatch's Monticello was composed. Its story will tell of a ferryboat empire worth millions which developed from scratch in the brief span of seven years.

Harry E. Speas was a man who enjoyed taking his family for a Sunday drive. He lived in San Francisco but the hills across the Golden Gate beckoned to Harry Speas who accordingly directed the week-end jaunts to the playland of Marin. One Sunday evening in 1920, the Speas' family car was one of hundreds waiting in line to board the Northwestern Pacific's ferry at Sausalito. The railroad company carried automobiles strictly as a side issue since the handling of large numbers upset the regular passenger schedules which was their main concern. As each regular trip was made, the limited number of cars which could be accommodated was let on board and the occupants of the waiting vehicles became more and more impatient. Finally, the last trip was made and Harry Speas was still one of the several drivers who had been unable to get their cars aboard the ferry. The group clubbed together and offered to pay the crew for another trip but such an arrangement was highly irregular and could not be entered into without official sanction, something rather difficult to secure at two o'clock in the morning.

The motorists expressed rather unkindly thoughts but there was nothing that could be done about it, so off the group went to seek lodgings for the balance of the night. But Harry Speas didn't sleep because he had given birth to a tremendous idea — the creation and operation of an exclusive auto ferry! So while the others slept, he sat quietly and calmly worked out some of the details which would make his plan come true.

In 1920, Speas incorporated the Golden Gate Ferry Company to operate between Sausalito and San Francisco. The corporation was capitalized for $1,000,000 and obtained a franchise from the State Railroad Commission to operate a ferry line subject to the supervision and approval of the commission. Mr. Speas also obtained the right to sell stock in the ferry company but at that point his parade of progress came to a halt. He lacked three things: money, boats, and terminals. Attempts were made to lease property at the foot of Laguna and Buchanan Streets but the rentals were for a thousand dollars per month and more which was out of the question. Speas then went to all the people he thought could be of help; he devoted his entire and untiring energies to the job of getting his ferry going, but at every turn he met failure. Happily for the Golden Gate Ferry Company, Harry E. Speas did not give up.

At the time Speas was organizing the ferry corporation, there was a small ferry company operating on Carquinez Straits called the Rodeo - Vallejo Ferry Company. This ferry was commenced by Aven J. Hanford, a man of tremendous ability, who had fought his way to the fore against tremendous odds. He was born in Calaveras County, California, in 1886, and was forced to make his own way in the world from the age of fourteen, working as a carpenter, a restaurant keeper, and later as a groceryman. It was during his latter occupation that he met another food merchandiser, Oscar H. Klatt, and the two of them saw possibilities in operating an auto ferry across Carquinez Straits. Klatt and Hanford formed a partnership and founded the Rodeo - Vallejo Ferry Company. They commenced operation in 1918 with the tiny steamer *Issaquah*, a boat constructed in Seattle in 1914. The venture was an immediate success and the partners accumulated much capital in two years.

But "Somebody," it seems, always has to come along just when things are going well and spoil a good thing. A group of Vallejo men, seeing the brilliant rise of the Rodeo - Vallejo ferry, built a causeway to Morrow Cove on the straits and a terminal in Crockett on the opposite shores. This group, headed by Forbes H. Brown and C. V. Stewart, had acquired the former Key System ferryboat *San Jose* which had been involved in an accident in 1919 and had been rebuilt as an automobile ferry. This ferry company was known as the "Six-Minute Ferry," so-called because of the length of time it took for the ferry to cross Carquinez Straits, and was something of an outgrowth of the Mare Island Ferry Company.

The Mare Island line, operating from Vallejo to Mare Island, had been controlled by many different interests in its time, even including ownership by the Aden Brothers, and had run a number of ferryboats over a period of years but the nucleus of the fleet was the *Vallejo* which had been built in Portland, Oregon, in 1879. The Mare Island Company carried workers from the mainland to Mare Island Navy Yard and, in times when the yard was engaged in carrying out an expanded shipbuilding program, the ferry line prospered. Its owners of 1918 and 1919, realizing tremendous profits from the two-way parade of war and postwar workers at the yard, had accumulated enough money to build the line to compete with Hanford and his Rodeo - Vallejo Ferry. The Six-Minute Ferry, by reason of their shorter route and larger boat, soon took away Hanford's lucrative business.

The Six-Minute Ferry then ordered the building of three new auto ferries at the Union Iron Works and leased property in Oakland with the intention of operating a ferry competitive to the Southern Pacific's. The growth of the Six-Minute Ferry had been much too meteoric to long ignore and the Southern Pacific took due and proper notice. They had not objected to the Carquinez service rendered by the Six-Minute line but a competing ferry from Oakland to San Francisco was a little too drastic.

Hanford too had begun to fight back. In 1921, he contracted with James Robertson of Alameda to build a screw propeller steam ferryboat using the machinery removed from the destroyer *Farragut* when the latter was scrapped at Mare Island. The new boat, 175 feet long, could carry sixty-four autos. The vessel had two stacks, one at each end of the upper deck in contrast to either a single stack or two stacks opposite each other in the middle of the upper deck. The ship was of wooden construction and was named the *Aven J. Hanford.* With this vessel, Hanford expected to compete favorably with the Six-Minute Ferry Company, but he never dreamed that the battle would be won as easily as it later was. In the winter of 1921-22, an earth slide at Morrow Cove put the Six-Minute Ferry completely out of operation and the company never recovered from the blow. The Rodeo - Vallejo Ferry immediately resumed prosperous operation and bought out its rival for $400,000 in March, 1922, the purchase price including the Mare Island Ferry Company as the wholly-owned subsidiary of the Rodeo - Vallejo operation.

On March 20, 1922, the *Aven J. Hanford* made its initial run from Vallejo to Rodeo — and Hanford and Klatt were back in the clover of prosperous business! To complete the demolition of the Six-Minute company, the Southern Pacific purchased the three new boats the former had ordered while the vessels were still on the ways and named them the *San Mateo,* the *Shasta,* and the *Yosemite.*

At about the time that Hanford and his associates were in the middle of their fight with the Six-Minute Ferry, Harry E. Speas decided that the only way for the dormant Golden Gate Ferry Company to get into operation was to obtain the help of experienced ferrymen. He went to Hanford and Klatt and offered to include them on the directorate of the Golden Gate Ferry. To Hanford and his associates this looked like a most attractive proposition, in view of their current operational problem for, should they lose their business on the Rodeo - Vallejo run completely, the boats could be trans-

The twin-stacked steamer *Aven J. Hanford* inaugurated the storybook Golden Gate Ferry service on May 28, 1922, between Sausalito and San Francisco. Her machinery and boilers came from the destroyer *Farragut*.

ferred to the Sausalito - San Francisco run. Accordingly, Aven Hanford became president of the Golden Gate Ferry Company, Harry Speas became vice-president and general manager, and Oscar Klatt was appointed treasurer.

Speas continued to diligently promote the ferry's fiscal affairs, trying to raise capital and secure land for his terminals. He finally obtained a satisfactory lease on some property at the foot of Hyde Street in San Francisco, for which he was obligated only to the extent of $250 per month. This left only the Sausalito terminal to arrange but again he met heavy opposition. The Northwestern Pacific Railroad was bucking him, now that his apparently impossible company had become a reality, and the citizens of Sausalito were up in arms over the prospect of a second auto ferry bringing additional automobile traffic to their quiet narrow streets.

A favorable, and possibly the only then available site, had quietly been bought up by a Sausalito sea captain, Randolph Petterson, who correctly expected that he would eventually have to be approached by the Golden Gate Ferry interests from whom he would logically be able to secure a good price. His expectation proved correct for Speas finally had to try to secure a lease from Petterson. The latter would have nothing to do with a lease, standing only for an outright sale of the property. Speas explained that the ferry company had no money of its own with which to buy the land and that Aven Hanford would purchase it for the company with his own funds. Petterson countered that his fellow townspeople would not think well of

Miss Marileah Speas christens the *Golden Gate* at James Robertson's Alameda yard. Standing directly behind Miss Speas is Aven J. Hanford, to the right and next to Hanford is Oscar Klatt, while Harry E. Speas is second from right.

SOUTHERN PACIFIC PHOTO

The *Golden Gate* was the first diesel-electric ferry on San Francisco Bay. The success experienced with the vessel led to the building of fourteen other vessels with this type of drive.

him if he sold the land to the ferry company in view of his neighbors' opposition to the ferry in the first place, so Hanford and Klatt bought the land
in the name of an employee of the Rodeo - Vallejo Ferry Company, thus
satisfying Petterson and the sale was completed.

With the last hurdle cleared, the Rodeo - Vallejo Ferry Company leased
the *Aven J. Hanford* to the Golden Gate Ferry Company for a ten-months
period, and the struggling little auto ferry, destined to become the largest
ferry company in the world, was ready to begin operation. Oddly enough,
the site of the new ferry landing in Sausalito was within a hundred feet of
the Sausalito Land & Ferry Company dock of 1868, where the little *Princess* had inaugurated Sausalito ferry service over fifty years before. In a
blue uniform and gold-trimmed cap, Captain John Lorentzen rang down
on the telegraph to the engine room on May 28, 1922, the old engine of the
U.S.S. *Farragut* throbbed away, and the Golden Gate Ferry started out on
its gold-laden trail.

Hanford and Speas proved themselves more than adequate to the business
challenge the new venture posed. Farsightedness had prompted them to
commence the building of a second ferry even before the actual service had
been initiated with the first boat. The second ship was also of wooden construction and was built at the highly-regarded Alameda shipyard of James
Robertson. Christened the *Golden Gate* by Mr. Speas' daughter, the
ferry was the first diesel-driven ferry on San Francisco Bay, having Werks-
poor type engines built by the Pacific Diesel Engine Company. Nearly all
the Golden Gate ferries were diesel driven and all of the diesel type
engines used an electric drive to supply the actual motive power with the
exception of one boat.

The *Golden Gate* went into the twenty-minute run from Sausalito to
Hyde Street in San Francisco on July 4, 1922, and immediately began to
"pack 'em in." The company bought the *Aven J. Hanford* outright, leaving the former Six-Minute Ferry *San Jose* to handle the traffic on the
Rodeo - Vallejo Ferry, and a third vessel, the *Golden West*, another diesel
driven vessel, was built by James Robertson in 1923. Auto traffic continued
to increase, the runs of the Golden Gate Ferry were extended to an all-day
all-night operation, and the revenue rolled in.

Hanford sold the Mare Island Ferry to one of his former employes on
June 1, 1923, the progressive Aven J. suddenly realizing that bridges were
paramount to ferries, and he built the first of the great bridges in the San
Francisco Bay area while still an important member of three ferry companies. This was the Antioch Bridge, extending from Antioch to Sherman
Island in the San Joaquin delta area. And shortly after its completion,
another company filed an application with the State to bridge Carquinez
Straits, a project which would have put the Rodeo - Vallejo Ferry Company
completely out of business.

In the interests of the stockholders of the Rodeo - Vallejo Ferry, Hanford
filed an application for a franchise to build the bridge and, after a stiff battle, secured the necessary enfranchisement. He and Oscar Klatt then incor-

Third boat of the Golden Gate Ferry was the *Golden West,* built by James Robertson in 1923. She was later sold and rebuilt as the *North Island* on the San Diego - Coronado Ferry.

Rebuilt from the Key System's first *Yerba Buena,* the *Harry E. Speas* was named for the Golden Gate Ferry's general manager and was later rechristened *Golden Coast.*

RALPH DEMORO PHOTO

The *Golden State,* built in 1926 at General Engineering & Dry Dock Company, had four sisters, the *Golden Age, Golden Bear, Golden Poppy,* and *Golden Shore.*

porated the American Toll Bridge Company in 1923, hired Professor Charles Derleth, Jr., dean of the University of California's College of Engineering, as engineer, and went to work. The bridge was completed in May, 1927, and immediately opened to traffic. Unfortunately, Aven J. Hanford was not there to witness the opening ceremonies, having passed away as the result of a stroke in 1926 at the age of but forty years. His short life, however, had been crowded with achievement, his bridges remaining as everlasting monuments to his resourcefulness.

Aven J. Hanford had sold his interests in the Golden Gate Ferry in March, 1925, having been succeeded as president by A. O. Stewart. The company had continued to expand, had leased the *Yerba Buena* (the first vessel bearing that name) from the Key System, converting her to an auto ferry and christening her the *Harry E. Speas.* Changes were made in the struggling *Hanford,* for the old destroyer's engines were not too successful For one thing, they had been built to operate in but one direction and the backup crosshead guides were of very light construction; consequently, the engines became considerably overheated when running in reverse for an entire trip, so the Golden Gate Ferry ordered the ship backed out of the slip, turned around, and operated in the forward direction only. This was, of course, a strange practice to pursue with a double-end boat so the company decided to junk the steam engines and replace them with diesel engines. This done, the boat was renamed the *Golden City,* and she returned to her run as a direct diesel-driven ship on April 22, 1927. Two short days later, the ferry was returning to Sausalito with only three cars aboard since it was a Sunday night and northbound traffic was generally light. It was foggy in the channel and suddenly appeared the steamer *Newport* which rammed the *Golden City* so sharply and placed her so out of control that the passengers and crew had barely five minutes in which to effect an escape from the sinking ship. The newsstand attendant managed to save the cash register and that was the only souvenir of the ill-fated *Golden City*, nee *Aven J. Hanford*. The rechristened ship had but a short life, although she was a famous vessel in the auto ferry days of San Francisco.

Other than this unfortunate sinking, 1927 was a great year for the Golden Gate Ferry Company. Three new routes were added: The Monticello Steamship Company line from San Francisco to Vallejo; the Hyde Street - Berkeley ferry route which necessitated the building of a three and a half mile wharf extending out in the Bay from the foot of Berkeley's University Avenue; and the building of an automobile toll road from Sears Point to Vallejo, a link saving many miles of travel on the North Bay route to Sacramento. Three more Key Route boats were leased: the *San Francisco,* which became the *Golden Dawn;* the *Claremont,* which became the *Golden Way;* and the *Fernwood,* which became the *Golden Era.* And, in addition, the ferry line added four new diesel-electric boats built by General Engineering & Drydock Company and powered by Rathbun-Jones diesel engines, three such engines driving generators and two electric motors. The electric equipment for these three ships, by way of a supply note, was of Westinghouse manufacture. First of the vessels was the *Golden State,* built one year earlier than the other three, and placed in service on the Fourth of July, 1926. The three other vessels which swelled the bright yellow fleet of the Golden Gate were the *Golden Bear, Golden Poppy,* and the *Golden Shore.* The *Harry E. Speas* was renamed the *Golden Coast* to keep in harmony with the names of the other vessels. In 1928, the rapidly expanding company opened a ferry line from Point Richmond to the Ferry Building in San Francisco and ordered the construction of still another diesel-electric ferry at the General Engineering yards, the *Golden Age.*

With four ferry routes on the Bay, the Southern Pacific and its allied companies became alarmed at the growth of the Golden Gate Ferry. The Southern Pacific had built the *El Paso, Klamath,* and the *New Orleans* to add to its Oakland and Alameda routes, but these three additions were not enough. So contracts were let for the construction of six fine boats, three for the Southern Pacific and three for the Northwestern Pacific.

The railroads now began to cater to the auto business they had all but shunned not too many years before and with the beautiful modern steel-hulled *Lake Tahoe, Fresno,* and *Stockton* with their New London Shipbuilding & Engine Company diesels, the Southern Pacific made a decided bid to regain the East Bay auto traffic. The Northwestern had three sister ships, the *Santa Rosa,* the *Mendocino,* and the *Redwood Empire,* all bidding for supremacy in the Marin ferry business but all playing to more or

Built for the Six-Minute Ferry and bought on the ways by the Southern Pacific, the *San Mateo*, built by the Union Iron Works, finally became Golden Gate Ferry property in the merger of 1929. She had two sisters, *Yosemite* and *Shasta*.

The *New Orleans*, together with her two sisters, the *Klamath* and the *El Paso*, were the last of the steam-driven auto ferries built for the Southern Pacific.

The *Lake Tahoe* (above) and her two sisters, the *Fresno* and the *Stockton,* were built for the Southern Pacific. The *Mendocino* (below) and her two sisters, the *Santa Rosa* and the *Redwood Empire,* were built for the Northwestern Pacific. These six vessels became the property of the Southern Pacific Golden Gate Ferries, Ltd., at the time of their merger in 1929.

less empty houses, so to speak. The Speas company had the cream of the business and the Southern Pacific far from succeeded in luring the public back aboard their decks with the de luxe diesel queens.

Negotiations were therefore undertaken between the two companies to form a joint auto ferry and a new corporation titled the Southern Pacific Golden Gate Ferries, Limited, was formed in 1929. The new company controlled nine routes, had a fleet of twenty-eight boats, and enjoyed an ever-increasing prosperity beginning with the commencement of the new service in May, 1929, which was not deterred until the Golden Gate and San Francisco - Oakland Bay bridges were completed.

The Berkeley and Richmond ferries bowed out in 1936, to be followed in 1937 by the Vallejo Route. Thus quietly and almost insignificantly the empire of Monticello and Zephaniah Jefferson Hatch ceased its operations without fanfare, the glory days of the *Asbury Park* and the *Florida* steaming up Mare Island Channel after their sea journeys from the Atlantic never again to be experienced.

Doggedly, the Sausalito - Hyde Street route and the Oakland Pier auto ferries survived, the Sausalito run surrendering to the supremacy of the Golden Gate Bridge in July, 1938, and a year later the Oakland auto ferry line called it a day. It seems that fate always dwelled in sentiment when ferries ceased operations on San Francisco Bay, and there was no exception to the rule in the case of the Golden Gate Ferry. Captain Edward Hallin had started as a deckhand on the *Aven J. Hanford* in 1922 and had risen to

First Officer Carl C. Nielsen and Captain Edward Hallin of the ferry *Yosemite* posed in the pilot house just before making the last trip of the Southern Pacific Golden Gate Ferry on the San Francisco - Sausalito run, July 24, 1938.

a captaincy on the *Golden State*. He was in command of the *Yosemite* on the last trip to Sausalito, and he was the captain on the final auto ferry trip to Oakland Pier, with the *Lake Tahoe*.

There were a lot of ferryboats for sale on San Francisco Bay when the Southern Pacific Golden Gate Ferries stopped running. The steamer *Yosemite*, originally built for the Six-Minute Ferry, was sold to a Uruguay ferry company, boarded up, and steamed down to Montevideo on the Rio de la Plata for the thirty three mile trip between Buenos Aires and Montevideo.

The *Golden Age* and the *Golden State* went to the Kitsap County Transportation Company in Seattle, Washington. The Puget Sound Navigation Company, flying the houseflag of the Blackball Line, got the *Shasta, San Mateo, Golden Poppy, Golden Shore, Lake Tahoe, Mendocino, Redwood Empire, Stockton, Santa Rosa, Fresno,* and, during the years of World War II, the *City of Sacramento* and the *Napa Valley*. The *Calistoga* and the steam *Golden* class boats were scrapped.

The Rodeo - Vallejo Ferry ceased operations upon completion of the Carquinez auto bridge but for many years the city of Martinez operated the *Issaquah* and the *City of Seattle* from Martinez to Benicia. These vessels were eventually replaced by former Richmond - San Rafael ferry boats. Only scant auto ferry lines operate on San Francisco Bay today, but to the Hatch Brothers, Aven Hanford, and Harry Speas belongs the credit for the transportation of automobiles by water to meet the demand for more efficient service than that which could be secured by long miles around the Bay instead of the short water miles, a demand which grew up in the days prior to the age of the cable-spun crossings.

CHAPTER VII

TWILIGHT OF THE FERRYBOAT

HE FERRYBOAT has had its day on the inland water-ways of California. Its era reaches far into the past, knows only the unpredictable future. A bay once alive with the thud of paddles laps restlessly at a shore which once was dotted with ferry wharves. At this writing, all of the routes save three have vanished and the setting sun silhouettes a scant few of the ferry queens which once ruled the Bay of San Francisco.

Of the passenger lines, only the Southern Pacific ferry from Oakland Pier to the Ferry Building in San Francisco remains. The other two ferries are operated for automobile traffic: one operated by the city of Martinez from Martinez to Benicia; the other, the Richmond - San Rafael Ferry & Transportation Company operating from Point San Quentin on the Marin shore to Point Molate on the Richmond side. The latter is by far the larger of the two companies and very much a veteran in the field of auto ferries. An intriguing story of a boy with an idea which haunted him until he saw his dream through to reality — that is the story behind the story of the Richmond - San Rafael Ferry. The same adventurous spirit that drove Z. J. Hatch, that haunted Harry E. Speas, that brought the great empire of Aven J. Hanford into being — that was the moving force behind the founding of the Richmond - San Rafael Ferry, born on a shoestring and finally developed into a prosperous enterprise.

Young Raymond H. Clarke was a San Rafael boy who loved to go fishing. He still does, for that matter. Since his retirement from the ferry company, he has developed the San Pablo Yacht Harbor where, amidst a breakwater of old steam schooners and the last remains of the ferryboat *Golden Gate,* he's still spinning a few yarns and going fishing. But back in 1911, Ray Clarke used to charter and skipper small fishing boats from San Rafael, taking private groups to the Marin Islands, Red Rock, and other favorite spots, often rounding out the day with a picnic at Point Richmond.

It was while on one of these outings that a dust-laden, overheated, chugging, horseless carriage of the era came to a jouncing halt on the circuitous road skirting Point Richmond, discharging a tired, miserable-appearing driver who immediately began to bubble questions about the land of promise he could see just three and one-half miles away across San Pablo Bay.

The little motorship *Issaquah* saw service for the Rodeo - Vallejo Ferry, the Martinez - Benicia Ferry and the Mare Island Ferry in her many years of faithful operation on the Bay.

Answering all his questions, Clarke pointed out that to get to Marin from Point Richmond, the driver would have to go all the way to the foot of Broadway in Oakland, take a ferry to San Francisco, then re-embark on a Northwestern Pacific boat to Sausalito. "A good seven-hour round trip — if you make connections," concluded Clarke. The driver lost all interest in Marin and any trip to the northern shores of the Golden Gate but Clarke encountered more and more like him every time he fished at Richmond.

The questions of the autoists intrigued Clarke, setting him to thinking about the possibility of a ferry with its financial reward to an operator with foresight. But, unfortunately, he lacked the capital necessary to inaugurate such a venture. He talked with some of the more prominent people in San Rafael, people who had known him most of his life, people who patiently listened to the boy's dreams as he unfolded his story to them, but people who assured him that such an enterprise would never succeed.

Raymond H. Clarke, however, was not one to give up his plan at discouragement's first signs. He next called on the office of the steamboat inspectors and made some preliminary inquiries as to what would be necessary in the way of equipment. His first idea was to use a barge pulled by his own small power boat but he discovered that it was mandatory that the floating equipment carrying automobiles have its own motive power aboard, thereby ruling out his first plan. Obviously a ferryboat was the only answer. He took his scheme to some of the more prosperous business men in Richmond; he talked as hard and as well as he knew how; he campaigned for his idea with all the enthusiasm of a Judah or a Sutro; but he met the same reception with which he was greeted in San Rafael. The answer was still "No!"

Although temporarily defeated, Clarke still talked "ferry" to anyone who was willing to listen and to a few who weren't. One Fourth of July, he even went so far as to set himself up on the Broadway wharf of the Southern Pacific in Oakland in order to take a personal poll of the automobiles awaiting their turn to board the San Francisco Auto Ferry. He asked each driver where he had come from, where he was bound for, and other questions necessary to establish the need for a Richmond - San Rafael ferry beyond the shadow of a doubt. Most of the drivers were annoyed at being queried by an inquisitive young man who was apparently not officially connected with the ferry company. They refused to answer questions, became rude, threatened violence — until they found out that he proposed to establish a ferry line between Richmond and San Rafael. Many apologized, expressed their interest, and one hundred and forty-five of the drivers stated that, had there been a ferry in operation that day between the two ferryless terminals, they would have taken it in preference to the necessarily more circuitous route. One hundred and forty-five cars per day meant that there was sufficient business to make the operation profitable. Ray Clarke's dream needed only the realization.

In 1914, Clarke had gone to live with an uncle by marriage, Charles Van Damme. Mr. Van Damme was quite a prominent business man in San Francisco, having operated a drayage firm there for some years. He had also been prominent in lumbering circles and had developed considerable timber acreage which had netted him a respectable profit and which had led him into partnership with Oliver J. Olson and Andrew F. Mahoney. These gentlemen had formed the firm of Olson & Mahoney Lumber Company, engaged in the coastwise traffic of transportation by lumber schooners. Mr. Van Damme was the experienced lumberman and the company's secretary, while Oliver Olson was a seagoing man and therefore handled the lumber schooners for the association. Andrew Mahoney acted as general factotum, with an eye for a sound business deal and a profitable one whenever one came about.

Mr. Van Damme lived for some months listening to his nephew's story of his fantastic automobile ferry. He remained immune to young Clarke's enthusiasm at first but gradually he began to absorb some of it himself. Even the partnership became mildly interested in the project but apparently never to the extent of plunging headlong into the venture. However, Mahoney came to Clarke one day and told him to start looking for a suitable boat. A dream had come true — years of talking to deaf ears, personal sacrifices, private investigations at personal expense — it all seemed worth while now.

Clarke first went to Sausalito to survey the *Grace Barton*. She had once run for the Adens and had raced the Monticello queens, but the sternwheeler was not suitable. Her main deck height was only eight feet, so

Clarke wisely set her aside for he was thinking of those big trucks he could haul for a good price and he required ample deck height.

The next scene of a search was Vallejo where the 328-ton *Ellen* of the Mare Island Ferry Company was idle, then not being used for the Vallejo commuter service. The little ship, built in 1883, seemed to be satisfactory and Clarke arranged with her owners, the Mare Island Employee's Association, to lease the boat at a rental of $250 per month. Some work had to be performed on her to accommodate automobiles but she would be available very shortly to the new company.

Commencing with an insignificant capitalization of $25,000, the ferry concluded leases for terminals on each side of the Bay. In Richmond, the site was located near Point Richmond close to where the rock quarry is now situated. On the Marin shore, the old North Pacific Coast wharf at Point San Quentin was leased from the Northwestern Pacific, which company was not using the wharf at the time and had not used it for some years. Completion of the details of incorporation was carried into effect upon the issuance of five thousand shares of stock at $100 per share. A few other necessary details were attended to — and the Richmond - San Rafael Ferry & Transportation Company was ready to do business.

Although Ray Clarke had promoted the ferry and had been one of its guiding hands, and although he had been quite an accomplished mariner on the Bay, his sailing was confined to small boats and hence he had no skipper's license. He spent his first three years with the ferry company as a deckhand but finally worked his way up to master in a very short time. The first crossing with Van Damme, Olson, and Mahoney on May 1, 1915, aboard the *Ellen,* saw Captain Hiram Knight at the wheel.

The *Ellen* was only 133 feet long, a side-wheeler with an engine which developed only 120 horsepower. It took almost an hour for the boat to make the crossing and she didn't make too many of them. On August 5, 1915, scarcely three months after service began, the *Ellen* failed to pass inspection by the steamboat inspection service — and the Richmond - San Rafael Ferry was temporarily out of business.

Ray Clarke again went shopping for another boat but it was soon concluded that the simplest expedient was to build a vessel which suited the needs of the traffic. At that time, James Robertson was operating an efficient shipyard in Benicia, building all types of wooden craft, and so he was commissioned to build a sidewheel wooden vehicular ferry for the company. The new ship was to be 152 feet long, was registered at 789 gross tons, and was powered by an engine built by C. H. Evans, developing 300 indicated horsepower. Captain Thomas Newsome of the Northwestern Pacific ferry was hired as the master of the new ferryboat which was named for Charles Van Damme and which served as the backbone of the San Rafael ferry fleet for a good many years.

A trial trip on a ferryboat operated by a new company is itself a very exciting thing, indeed; but a trial trip on a new ferryboat operated by a company that you yourself have organized out of your own dreams is some-

James Robertson, builder, and Charles Van Damme look over the ferryboat named for the latter as she was under construction at Robertson's shipyard in Benicia.

thing that few ever experience. It was therefore with justifiable jubilance that Ray Clarke set off down Market Street in San Francisco on July 23, 1916, for the *Charles Van Damme* was awaiting him at Pier 11 for her trial run. He very nearly didn't make it, though, for July 23 of that year was "Preparedness Day" and a patriotic parade was in progress. As Clarke arrived at the corner of Steuart and Market Streets, someone threw a bomb into the crowd watching and things happened. The who, why, and what of the bombing with its resulting jurisprudence has been the subject of great controversies in the annals of California crime, but Ray Clarke sped on uninjured for the Richmond - San Rafael Ferry was losing money every day it didn't have a boat in operation.

The trial trip was a success and the *Charles Van Damme* was soon plying the waters of the grey San Pablo Bay, upper arm of San Francisco Bay. Her capacity of forty-five automobiles was very gratifying after the Ellen's scant seventeen. Not only that but the *Van Damme* could make the crossing in half an hour. She left Richmond at 7:30, 9:30, and 11:30 a.m., and at 2:30, 4:30, and 6:30 p.m. Departures from Point San Quentin were made at 8:15 and 10:15 a.m. and at 12:15, 3:15, 5:15, and 7:15 p.m. This was the timecard as of December 3, 1917.

Although substantial polls had been taken by the ferry company prior to the commencement of service to ascertain the possibility of contemplated auto traffic, other prospective traffic had been overlooked. Pedestrians had not been taken into account nor had the cattle from Marin dairy ranches — but both patronized the ferry, the latter in hastily improvised pens constructed near the paddle boxes. "We never hired a deckhand who couldn't punch cows," declared Ray Clarke in later years.

Eventually Clarke earned his master's license and took command of the *Van Damme* and Captain Newsome returned to the Northwestern Pacific ferries. For Clarke, it was the complete fulfillment of his dream when he took command of his company's boat. He began a new cycle of service in his company, one which eventually led him to the port captaincy when that position was created. For many years, he navigated the route from the Contra Costa shore to the opposite landing in the shadow of San Quentin, one of the nation's largest penal institutions. The prison brought additional business to the little line, and deputy sheriffs from all over California became well acquainted with Captain Clarke as they brought their prisoners to San Quentin and returned home. They would frequently phone him from San Jose to say that the train had been delayed, if such were the case, and would he please hold the boat. Clarke thought nothing of holding the *Van Damme* for an extra half hour as the frantic deputy raced toward Point Richmond with his reluctant charge in tow.

"I've dined with the most desperate of criminals," said Captain Clarke, "men who had their last meal outside of prison on the restaurant of my boat. But the public officials who had contact with us never forgot the courtesies we extended them; our holding the ferry for them didn't do our company any harm."

The waters of San Pablo Bay are usually calm, for the channel is somewhat protected from the sea winds and fogs, making the area ideal for small boats. A crossing on the Richmond - San Rafael run is usually uneventful, one of charm to delight the traveler, a pleasant break in a sometimes wearisome journey. The morning of Christmas Day, 1921, was just like many another morning which broke on San Pablo Bay on an average of three hundred days out of the year. Captain Clarke left Point San Quentin with the *Van Damme* at 9:00 a.m., with twenty-five cars aboard, the limousine of San Quentin's warden among them. Before they had made much headway from the slip, a strong southeast gale broke upon the ferryboat — and the half day which followed was one which lasts forever in the memory of those unfortunate enough to have to experience it. The wind was so terrific that the vessel could not make any headway in its efforts to reach Red Rock. The strong seas broke the rudder loose and carried it away and the automobile deck became awash. Most of the passengers, scared half to death, strapped on life preservers and the machinery hatches had to be battened down to prevent the boat from being swamped. The vessel heeled over badly in the wind and sea, and Captain Clarke battled valiantly to save the ferry, for the company had no other boat and could ill-afford to lose this one, much less stand the tragedy of a sinking.

One farmer with an auto which was probably not worth more than fifty dollars in its condition was nevertheless very much concerned about the fate of his car. He surrounded it with life preservers and made emergency preparations to render it watertight. Fortunately, he never had the satisfaction of finding out the efficacy of his arrangements but he was certainly keeping busy. In the middle of all the confusion, the wind blew a lifeboat out of the davits and it fell down, smashing the warden's limousine. Up on the bridge, Captain Clarke was having his troubles for the stack guys had been carried away and the swaying of the stack was now working on the whistle cord, since the whistle sounded of its own accord with every new gust of wind. The wild melee was brought to a merciful ending when the *Van Damme* was brought to a successful anchorage off Winehaven at 2:00 that afternoon. The storm finally abated and the vessel was towed to the Richmond slip without further casualty. The ferry company never experienced another storm like that one and it is doubtful whether acquaintance with another such tempest would ever willingly be solicited. A tremendous amount of credit was due the crew for saving the ship and its load, for in the log books of many other ferry companies the simple entry was made: "Too rough to run today."

The *Charles Van Damme* had served to put the struggling infant company on its financial feet. She had carried the load alone and had more than justified Ray Clarke's persistence by making a modest profit for Olson and Mahoney. Although the ferry was a side issue with the lumbermen, its potentialities were not underestimated by them. The loads carried by the *Van Damme* showed that the business was definitely there and that additional business could be built up if the company had additional boats to serve the public.

The *City of Richmond* leaves the Richmond slip on a journey to Point San Quentin. These little sidewheelers were originally painted red, were trimmed in baby blue in the interior, and carried the chain-link symbol of the Richmond - San Rafael Ferry on each wheel house.

By 1921, the auto ferry business on San Francisco Bay was on a firm footing; the new companies, such as the Rodeo-Vallejo and the Six-Minute Ferries were solidly established and the embryo Golden Gate Ferry was on the sidelines ready to burst into reality — all of which added up to the fact that automobile ferryboats were at a premium in the locality. When the Richmon - San Rafael Ferry required a new boat, the only course open to the company was to build one. Since building the *Van Damme*, James Robertson had moved his shipyard from Benicia to Alameda, first to the foot of Grand Street and later to the site at Blanding Avenue between Regent and Broadway, at which locality this grand old boatbuilder was later to lose his life in a shipyard accident.

Robertson was awarded the contract in 1920 to build a new boat for the expanding of the "Great Red Fleet," a vessel named the *City of Richmond*, sixteen feet longer than the *Charles Van Damme*. The keel of the vessel was laid November 15, 1920, and she was launched in May of the following year. The *City of Richmond* was powered with an inclined cross-compound marine engine driving paddle wheels and developing 500 indicated horsepower which was 200 horsepower more than the tinier *Van Damme*.

With the addition of the new vessel, the ferry company was now able to double its schedule, a material aid on holidays and week ends when the boats hauled all the automobiles they could carry all day long. Next problem to solve was the shortening of the distance between terminals, for it had always been a sore point for the ferry company to have to journey along the Richmond shore all the way from Point Molate to Point Richmond when a terminal at Point Molate would materially shorten the route and make it possible for the company to give better service.

A purchase of the extensive properties adjoining and including Point Molate was consummated in 1924, the ferry line eventually disposing of all the land with the exception of that which is now the site of the present Richmond terminals. A satisfactory leasehold interest was negotiated for this property and the terminal was moved from Point Richmond to the Molate location.

During the same period, the company added another boat to the roster, for the ferry business was increasing annually at an increasing rate, a rate which has kept up continually since the inception of the line. Honoring the city at the opposite end of the run, the new vessel built at James Robertson's shipyard was named the *City of San Rafael*. Four feet longer than the *City of Richmond*, the wooden sidewheeler was powered with the engines from the old sternwheeler *Iroquois* which gave the *City of San Rafael* 650 horsepower, over twice the amount of output of the little *Charles Van Damme*. The keel for the *City of San Rafael* was laid on December 10, 1923, the vessel was launched on the 17th of May of the following year and delivered on June 21, 1924.

The addition of the *City of San Rafael* gave the Richmond - San Rafael Ferry a fleet of three vessels, and the strength of the company has always been at a minimum of three boats ever since. With all boats in service, the

ROY GRAVES PHOTO

The Point Molate terminal of the Richmond - San Rafael Ferry. The *Sonoma Valley*, the *Klamath*, the *City of San Rafael*, and the *City of Richmond* are lined up before the photographer's camera.

Once named *San Jose* and flying the flag of the Key System and then the Six-Minute Ferry, the *Sonoma Valley* rounded out her active career with the Rich-mond - San Rafael Ferry.

schedule called for a boat to leave each terminal every twenty minutes, while two boats could maintain a half-hourly schedule. Originally the boats operated only eight hours a day but demands have increased the service to sixteen hours a day. The company has not yet seen fit to operate on an all-night schedule such as that adopted by the Golden Gate ferry with its great volume of business.

A fourth boat was added in 1927 when the Carquinez Bridge spelled the finish of the Rodeo - Vallejo Ferry. This vessel was the veteran *San Jose,* originally built for the Key System and later rebuilt into an auto ferry by the Six-Minute group. When the Six-Minute Ferry was sold to the Rodeo - Vallejo interests, the *San Jose* went with the sale. Her name did not appeal to her new owners on the Richmond - San Rafael, so it was changed to the more appropriate *Sonoma Valley* soon after her purchase.

No further changes were made by the line for the next eleven years. San Pablo Bay mothered a good fleet and Red Rock looked down upon the red fleet which sailed by day after day, so faithfully linking the Marin shore with that of Contra Costa. Many families depended on the Richmond - San Rafael Ferry for their bread and butter, and of its faithful employees, there was none so proud to be in command of his boat than Captain Raymond H. Clarke. From his sweeping wheelhouse, he could still see that Richmond shore where the questions of traveling motorists had planted the seed of an idea in his mind, a seed that germinated into a comfortable and satisfying living for the ferry captain and an indispensable service to the public.

In July of 1938, the Southern Pacific - Golden Gate Ferries ceased their Sausalito - San Francisco service, leaving only the auto ferry from Oakland Pier to the Ferry Building. This left the large ferry concern with twenty-eight vessels and only a fifteen-minute run from Oakland to San Francisco on which to operate them. Consequently, the S.P. - Golden Gate operated the six steel diesel boats, the *Santa Rosa, Mendocino, Redwood Empire, Stockton, Fresno,* and *Lake Tahoe* on their last remaining run. Twenty-two boats went up for sale, and the Richmond - San Rafael Ferry got one of the finest windfalls ever to be realized by a ferry company. For approximately ten per cent of their value, the Richmond - San Rafael company was able to purchase three steel-hulled vessels with a capacity of seventy automobiles apiece, each boat able to hold about twice the capacity of the *Van Damme.*

The new boats were purchased in November, 1938, and they were the former *Klamath, El Paso,* and the *New Orleans.* Although graced with names peculiar to the operations of the Southern Pacific's rail lines, only one vessel was renamed when the *New Orleans* became the *Russian River.* The three vessels are the nucleus of the present fleet of the ferry company, their triple-expansion engines, single propellers at each end, and three water-tube boilers serving the needs of the Richmond - San Rafael Ferry in a most satisfactory manner.

The four veterans were promptly tied up, one being used as a spare when

The *El Paso* once left her wake between Oakland and San Francisco for Southern Pacific. Now she steams between Point San Quentin and the Richmond shore.

The steamer *Klamath* was purchased by the Richmond - San Rafael Ferry from the Southern Pacific Golden Gate Ferries. She still serves the Richmond line on grey San Pablo Bay.

the situation warranted it. The *Van Damme* had been the extra boat ever since the coming of the *Sonoma Valley* and she now became the standby boat. Out of sentiment, she was retained by the company for some years but an eventual sale was made to the city of Martinez and she was used on the Martinez-Benicia run. The *City of Richmond* was sold to the American Sardine Company and refitted as a fish reduction plant.

The *City of San Rafael* had a stormy ending with the Richmond line. She distinguished herself by being in a laid-up status just about as often as she was in operation. There was a big blow on the Bay in February, 1943, and it reached considerable proportions on San Pablo Bay in the vicinity of Point Molate. The wind blew hard and the seas mounted up while the tied-up ferryboats strained heavily on their mooring lines. On the *City of San Rafael,* the lines eventually parted, one by one, and the "corpse walked once again." With a tarpaulin over her stack, with boilers cold and engines stilled, the *City of San Rafael* drifted out into the channel, crewless and helpless on the storm-whipped San Pablo Bay.

When the ferry company realized that their child had escaped, when aid was solicited of the neighboring Standard Oil Company, when the latter responded by sending a tugboat, things were pretty much out of control. The crew of the tug managed to get a line on the ferryboat, but, when the line took its first strain, it parted, and the tempest lashed mercilessly at the *San Rafael* until she was finally deposited on the shore near Winehaven on a spot where only high tide and storm would float a vessel.

Considered a loss by her owners, the vessel was sold to a scrap dealer who made some attempts at junking her during the time he owned her; but World War II was raging, other business was more pressing, and the *City of San Rafael* was spared the ignominy of being scrapped. About that time, the Army Transportation Corps was looking for a ferryboat and they decided that the *City of San Rafael* was well worth the trouble of salvaging. Under the able direction of Captain Thomas Klitgaard, the work was commenced in September and consumed a month of hard toil.

First, the vessel was jacked up on blocks, and skids were constructed toward the water. But the waterline was an appalling distance away; to the laborers, it appeared that the Bay was visible from where the *City of San Rafael* was lodged only on a clear day. However, Mohammed not going to the Mountain, it was decided that the Mountain should go to Mohammed, this being accomplished in the present instance by a channel being dredged between the Bay and the stranded vessel. With bulldozers and caterpillar tractors, the channel was graded and a pond was built which was to float the *San Rafael.*

The skids were built to the water's edge and for a second time in her life the *City of San Rafael* faced a launching. This time it was to be accomplished with the aid of tractors. With a tractor pulling at the bow and another at the stern, the ferry started to move once more; but one tractor pulled more than the other, the vessel fell off the skids at one end, and the project had to be commenced again. Blocked up once more and reposi-

The *Russian River* was formerly the *New Orleans* of the Southern Pacific

The *Sierra Nevada* was rebuilt into an auto ferry in 1947. Her previous service was with the Western Pacific and the Southern Pacific and formerly carried the names *Edward T. Jeffery* and *Feather River.*

Not a builder's sideways launching, but a salvage on the Winehaven beach! The *City of San Rafael,* high and dry, is depicted being readied for refloating by the Army in September, 1943.

tioned, the ferry was readied a second time, and this one was successful. The operation cost $47,000 which was certainly a fair figure considering that the Army got a ferryboat out of it.

But almost immediately the *City of San Rafael* proved to be too small for the Army's needs, being replaced by the *Catalina* and the *Cabrillo* of the Wilmington Transportation Company. So the *City of San Rafael* was eventually purchased by the city of Martinez and now operates for that line along with her running mate, the *Charles Van Damme.*

In 1947, the Richmond - San Rafael Ferry & Transportation Company added another boat to their fleet which they purchased on May 30 of that year. She was the *Sierra Nevada,* one of the most transferred of boats on the Bay. Beginning life as the *Edward T. Jeffrey* of the Western Pacific, the vessel was renamed the *Feather River,* sold to the Southern Pacific to be rechristened the *Sierra Nevada,* leased in turn to the Key System and the Shipyard Ferries, until she was finally taken over by the Richmond - San Rafael Ferry and converted to carry automobiles.

This sturdy little band of ferryboats, the *Russian River,* the *El Paso,* the *Klamath* and the *Sierra Nevada* now comprise the fleet which shuttles between Point Molate and San Quentin. Somewhere during the early Thirties, the color scheme of the vessels was changed from red with white lettering to white with black letters to conform to the usual color standards on San Francisco Bay. During World War II, the general offices of the company were removed from the suite of the Olson, Mahoney Lumber

Company in San Francisco to Point Molate where, almost any time during the week you can find Mr. Oliver J. Olson, Jr., holding down the polished desk of the president of the Richmond - San Rafael Ferry Company. His is the last of the large automobile ferry lines on the Bay but its future too is something in the shape of a question mark for a Richmond - San Rafael bridge has been a topic of discussion among civic leaders for some years. Undoubtedly, the bridge will eventually be built, the only question being, "How soon?"

The Clarkes, the Hanfords, the Hatches, the Minturns, the Donahues, and the others who founded the great ferry companies of San Francisco Bay performed a public service which cannot be measured in dollars and cents. Their achievements extending over a century of progress in San Francisco and environs should always be remembered as one of the more important contributions to the growth and development of the great communities bordering San Francisco Bay.

Their ferryboats were endeared to the throngs who knew them; the boats were the friends of the travelers who rode them, as much a part of their daily life as their homes, their businesses, and the throbbing communities in which they resided. Besides those who used the boats daily, there were many of San Francisco's regular visitors who felt that no trip to the city was complete without a ferryboat ride, that no approach to any city was more beautiful, more enchanting, more lasting in memory.

For the trim white boats which remain, the present years are truly the twilight of the ferryboat. The chance of increasing numbers of ferries is doubtful, the chance of total elimination is large. They plod their toilsome way in the shadows of the bridges which destroyed their sisters and, amid a fading era another attribute in a vanishing chain is disappearing from the charm of the City by the Golden Gate.

That the performance of a great and necessary duty has been faithfully fulfilled cannot at any time be doubted; that a growing city relied on walking beams and paddle wheels for much of its progress is acclaimed without dispute; and that the ferryboat gave its all to do a job that cannot receive too great a commendation is a tribute to the ferrymen who helped build their San Francisco.

ROSTER OF FERRY VESSELS

NAME FORMER NAME OPERATOR	HULL TYPE	LENGTH BREADTH DEPTH GROSS TONS	BUILDER – DATE ENGINE BUILDER BOILER MFG.	TYPE ENGINE SIZE HORSEPOWER TYPE BOILER	REMARKS
ALAMEDA — S.F. & ALAMEDA R.R. CO CENTRAL PACIFIC	WOOD SIDE WHEEL	195'- 0" — — 813	———— 1866 ———— ————	I CYL. VERT. BEAM — 350 I BOILER	
ALAMEDA — SOUTHERN PACIFIC	STEEL SIDE WHEEL	293'-0" 42.2' R — 2302	S. P. CO. 1913 S. P. CO. ————	2-2 CYL. COMP. 20"X 40"X 96" 1980 4 WATER TUBE	
AMADOR — CENTRAL PACIFIC	WOOD SIDE WHEEL	199'-0" — — 897	———— 1869 ———— ————	— — 300 —	
ARROW — MONTICELLO S.S. CO	WOOD SINGLE END SINGLE SCREW	147'-0" R 22'-6" R 9'- 3" 318	———— 1903 ———— ————	3 CYL. TRIPLE 14"X 21.5"X 35"X — 1000 I BOILER	
AVEN J. HANFORD GOLDEN GATE FERRY RODEO – VALLEJO FERRY	WOOD SINGLE SCREW	176.8' R 30.5' R — 353	J. ROBERTSON 1922 MACHINERY AND BOILERS FROM DESTROYER "FARRAGUT"	4 CYL. TRIPLE 20½"29½"30½"30½"18" 900 2 WATER TUBE	RENAMED GOLDEN CITY
BAY CITY — SOUTH PACIFIC COAST R.R. SOUTHERN PACIFIC	WOOD SIDE WHEEL	247'-0" 66'- I" 15'- 0" 1283	———— 1878 ———— ————	I CYL. VERT. BEAM 52" X 144" 860 2 SCOTCH MARINE	
BERKELEY — CENTRAL PACIFIC SOUTHERN PACIFIC	STEEL SCREW	279'-0" 40'-3" R 14'- I" 1883	UNION IRON WORKS 1898 UNION IRON WORKS UNION IRON WORKS	3 CYL. TRIPLE 22"X 34"X 56"X 36" 1450 2 SINGLE END	
CALISTOGA EX – FLORIDA S. P. G.G. FERRY MONTICELLO S.S. CO.	STEEL SCREW	298'-0" 45'-0" R 16'- I" 2680	MARYLAND STEEL 1907 ———— ————	4 CYL. TRIPLE 24½"40½"47½"47½"42 2600 4 SINGLE END	
CAZADERO — NORTHWESTERN PACIFIC NORTH SHORE R.R.	WOOD SIDE WHEEL	256'- 0" 68'- 0" 17'-0" 1682	J. DICKIE 1903 RISDON IRON WORKS ————	I CYL. VERT. BEAM 56" X 144" 1600 2 DRYBACK	
CHARLES VAN DAMME — RICHMOND-SAN RAFAEL FERRY	WOOD SIDE WHEEL	152'-0" R 36'-10" R — 789	J. ROBERTSON 1916 C. H. EVANS ————	2 CYL. COMP. 16"X 20"X 54" 300 2 BOILERS	
CITY OF RICHMOND — RICHMOND-SAN RAFAEL FERRY	WOOD SIDE WHEEL	168'-0" R 34'-0" R — 408	J. ROBERTSON 1921 UNION MACHINE CO. ————	2 CYL.CROSS COM 18"X 36"X 72" 500 —	
CITY OF SACRAMENTO EX-ASBURY PARK S. P. G.G. FERRY MONTICELLO S.S. CO.	STEEL TWIN SCREW	297'-0" 50'-0" R 15'- 5" 3016	WM. CRAMP & SONS 1903 WM. CRAMP & SONS ROBERTSON	2 4CYL TRIPLES 23½"37½"43"43½"30" 5900 9 WATER TUBE	
CITY OF SAN RAFAEL — RICHMOND – SAN RAFAEL FERRY	WOOD SIDE WHEEL	172'-0" R 36'-9" R — 484	J. ROBERTSON 1924 MACHINERY FROM STERN-WHEELER "IROQUOIS"	2 CYL. COMP. 20"X 44"X 72" 650 2 BOILERS	
CITY OF SEATTLE — CITY OF MARTINEZ	WOOD SIDE WHEEL	121'-6" R 38'- 4" R 8'-6" 196	———— 1888 ———— ————	I CYL. 16"X 60" 270 I RET. TUBE	BUILT PORTLAND, OREGON
CLAREMONT — KEY SYSTEM	WOOD SINGLE SCREW	189'-0" R 38'-0" R 19'-3" 672	JOHN W. DICKIE 1907 ———— ————	2 CYL. DBL.COMP. 20"X 42" X 28" 2000 2 WATER TUBE	RENAMED GOLDEN WAY
CONTRA COSTA — CONTRA COSTA ST. NAV. CO.	WOOD SIDE WHEEL	170'-0" — — 449	JOHN G. NORTH 1857 ———— ————	I CYL.VERT BEAM — 150 —	
CONTRA COSTA — SOUTHERN PACIFIC	STEEL SIDE WHEEL	.433'-0" 67'-3" R 19'-10" 5373	SOUTHERN PACIFIC 1914 S. P. CO. ————	2-2 CYL. COMP. 60" X 96" 3000 8 WATER TUBE	
EL CAPITAN — CENTRAL PACIFIC	WOOD SIDE WHEEL	194'-0" R 62'-8" 14'-0" 982	———— 1868 ———— ————	I CYL.VERT. BEAM 36"X 144" 365 4 RETURN TUBE	

NAME FORMER NAME OPERATOR	HULL TYPE	LENGTH BREADTH DEPTH GROSS TONS	BUILDER – DATE ENGINE BUILDER BOILER MFG.	TYPE ENGINE SIZE HORSEPOWER TYPE BOILER	REMARKS
ELLEN — RICHMOND–SAN RAFAEL FERRY MARE ISLAND FERRY	WOOD SIDE WHEEL	133'–0" R 24'–9" R 7'–5" 328	— 1883 — —	— 120 —	BUILT AT VALLEJO BROKEN UP 1919
EL PASO — RICHMOND–SAN RAFAEL FERRY S. P. G. G. FERRY	STEEL SINGLE SCREW	234'–0" R 44'–11" R — 1953	UNION IRON WORKS 1924 BUCKEYE ENG. CO. TRAYLOR ENG. CO.	3 CYL. TRIPLE 19"X 32"X 56" X 36" 1400 3 WATER TUBE	
ENCINAL — SOUTH PACIFIC COAST R. R. SOUTHERN PACIFIC	WOOD SIDE WHEEL	274'–0" 72'–6" 15'–10" 2014	— 1888 — —	I CYL. VERT. BEAM 52" X 144" 972 4 SCOTCH MARINE	
EUREKA — SOUTHERN PACIFIC NORTHWESTERN PACIFIC	WOOD SIDE WHEEL	299'–6" 78'–6" 14'–2" 2420	SOUTHERN PACIFIC 1922 FULTON IRON WORKS —	I CYL. VERT. BEAM 65" X 144" 1500 4 DRYBACK	REBUILT FROM UKIAH
FEATHER RIVER EX–EDWARD T. JEFFREY WESTERN PACIFIC R. R. CO.	STEEL SINGLE SCREW	218'–0" R 42'–0" R — 1578	MOORE & SCOTT 1913 — —	2–2 CYL. COMP. 20" X 42" X 28 2500 4 WATER TUBE	RENAMED SIERRA NEVADA
FERNWOOD — KEY SYSTEM	WOOD SINGLE SCREW	194'–4" R 38'–0" R 19'–3" 673	JOHN W. DICKIE 1907 — —	2 - 2 CYL. COMP. 20" X 42" X 28" 2000 2 WATER TUBE	RENAMED GOLDEN ERA
FRESNO — S. P. G. G. FERRY SOUTHERN PACIFIC	STEEL SINGLE SCREW	251'–0" R 46'–3" R 19'–2" 2468	UNION IRON WORKS 1927 NEW LONDON S.B. & E. AND GENERAL ELECTRIC —	4 DIESEL 2 ELECT. MOTORS 1250	RENAMED WILLAPA PUGET SOUND NAV. CO.
GARDEN CITY — SOUTHERN PACIFIC SOUTH PACIFIC COAST R. R.	WOOD SIDE WHEEL	243'–0" 66'–6" 15'–7" 1080	— 1879 — —	I CYL. VERT. BEAM 46" X 144" 933 2 SCOTCH MARINE	
GENERAL FRISBIE — MONTICELLO S. S. CO.	WOOD SINGLE SCREW	187'–0" R 29'–0" R 11'–11" 670	G. R. WHIDDEN 1900 UNITED ENGINEERING —	4 CYL. TRIPLE 16½ 26½ 30½ 30½ 24" 1000	
GOLDEN AGE — S. P. G. G. FERRY GOLDEN GATE FERRY	WOOD SINGLE SCREW	240'–0" 60'–0" 16' 9" 779	GENERAL ENG. CO. 1928 RATHBUN–JONES, ING- ERSOL–RAND TYPE & WESTINGHOUSE ELECT.	3 DIESEL 2 ELECT. MOTOR 950	RENAMED KLAHANIE KITSAP COUNTY TRANSPORTATION CO.
GOLDEN BEAR — S. P. G. G. FERRY GOLDEN GATE FERRY	WOOD SINGLE SCREW	240'–0" 60'–0" 15'–9" 779	GENERAL ENG. CO. 1927 RATHBUN–JONES, ING- ERSOL–RAND TYPE & WESTINGHOUSE ELECT.	3 DIESEL 2 ELECT. MOTORS 950	
GOLDEN CITY EX– AVEN J. HANFORD GOLDEN GATE FERRY	WOOD SINGLE SCREW	176'–9" R 30'–6" R — 353	JAMES ROBERTSON 1922 WASHINGTON ESTEP —	2 DIESEL — —	
GOLDEN COAST EX–HARRY E. SPEAS S. P. G. G. FERRY	WOOD SINGLE SCREW	200'–0" 60'–0" 17'–0" 616	JOHN DICKIE 1903 — —	3 CYL. TRIPLE 12"X 25" X 42" X 27 1200 2 WATER TUBE	
GOLDEN DAWN EX–SAN FRANCISCO S. P. G. G. FERRY GOLDEN GATE FERRY	WOOD SINGLE SCREW	202'–0" 60'–0" 18'–2" 612	JOHN DICKIE 1905 — —	2 - 2 CYL. COMP. 20" X 42" X 28" 2000 2 WATER TUBE	
GOLDEN ERA EX– FERNWOOD S. P. G. G. FERRY GOLDEN GATE FERRY	WOOD SINGLE SCREW	200'–0" 60'–0" 19'–2" 673	JOHN DICKIE 1907 — —	2 - 2 CYL. COMP. 20" X 42" X 28" 2000 2 WATER TUBE	
GOLDEN GATE — S. P. G. G. FERRY GOLDEN GATE FERRY	WOOD SINGLE SCREW	220'–0" 60'–0" 13'–5" 598	J. ROBERTSON 1922 PACIFIC DIESEL ENG., WERKSPOR TYPE AND GENERAL ELECTRIC	2 DIESEL 2 ELECT. MOTORS 1050	
GOLDEN POPPY — S. P. G. G. FERRY GOLDEN GATE FERRY	WOOD SINGLE SCREW	240'–0" 60'–0" 15'–5" 779	GENERAL ENGINEERING, 1927, RATHBUN–JONES, INGERSOL–RAND TYPE & WESTINGHOUSE ELECT.	3 DIESEL 2 ELECT. MOTORS 950 —	RENAMED CHETZEMOKA PUGET SOUND NAV. CO.
GOLDEN SHORE — S. P. G. G. FERRY GOLDEN GATE FERRY	WOOD SINGLE SCREW	240'–0" 60'–0" 15'–9" 779	GENERAL ENG. CO. 1927 RATHBUN – JONES, INGERSOL–RAND TYPE & WESTINGHOUSE ELECT.	3 DIESEL 2 ELECT. MOTORS 950 —	RENAMED ELWHA PUGET SOUND NAVIGATION CO.

NAME FORMER NAME OPERATOR	HULL TYPE	LENGTH BREADTH DEPTH GROSS TONS	BUILDER – DATE ENGINE BUILDER BOILER MFG.	TYPE ENGINE SIZE HORSEPOWER TYPE BOILER	REMARKS
GOLDEN STATE — S. P. G. G. FERRY GOLDEN GATE FERRY	WOOD SINGLE SCREW	240'-0" 60'-0" 13'-5" 780	GENERAL ENG. CO. 1926 PACIFIC DIESEL ENG. CO. WERKSPOR TYPE AND GENERAL ELECTRIC	3 DIESEL 2 ELECT. MOTORS 950 —	RENAMED KEHLOKEN, KITSAP COUNTY TRANSPORTATION CO.
GOLDEN WAY EX-CLAREMONT S. P. G. G. FERRY GOLDEN GATE FERRY	WOOD SINGLE SCREW	200'-0" 60'-0" 19' 0" 672	JOHN DICKIE 1907 — —	2-2 CYL. COMP. 20" X 42" X 28" 2000 2 WATER TUBE	
GOLDEN WEST — S. P. G. G. FERRY GOLDEN GATE FERRY	WOOD SINGLE SCREW	220'-0" 60'-0" 13'-0" 594	J. ROBERTSON 1923 PACIFIC DIESEL ENG. CO. WERKSPOR TYPE AND GENERAL ELECTRIC	2 DIESEL 2 ELECT. MOTORS 1300 —	REBUILT 1938 AS NORTH ISLAND CORONADO FERRY
HARRY E. SPEAS EX-YERBA BUENA GOLDEN GATE FERRY	WOOD SINGLE SCREW	200'-0" 60'-0" 17'-0" 616	JOHN W. DICKIE 1903 — —	3 CYL. TRIPLE 12"X25"X42"X27" 1200 2 WATER TUBE	RENAMED GOLDEN COAST
HAYWARD — KEY SYSTEM	■ STEEL SINGLE SCREW	225'-0" R 42'-0" R 19'-6" 1653	LOS ANGELES S.B. 1923 GENERAL ELECTRIC BABCOCK-WILCOX	STEAM TURBINE 2 ELECT. MOTORS 1350 2 WATER TUBE	
ISSAQUAH MARE ISLAND FERRY CITY OF MARTINEZ RODEO-VALLEJO FERRY	WOOD SINGLE SCREW	114'-5" R 38'-4" R 8'-10" 288	— — — 1914	DIESEL — 250 —	
JAMES M. DONAHUE — NORTHWESTERN PACIFIC S. F. & N. P. R. R.	WOOD SINGLE END SIDE WHEEL	227'-9" 55'-9" 9'-7" 730	WM. E. COLLYER 1875 QUINTARD IRON WORKS FULTON IRON WORKS	1 CYL. VERT. BEAM 48" X 132" 950 1 RETURN TUBE	
KLAMATH — RICHMOND-SAN RAFAEL FERRY S. P. G. G. FERRY	STEEL SINGLE SCREW	234'-0" R 44'-10" R 19'-5" 1952	UNION IRON WORKS 1925 NORDBERG MFG. CO. TRAYLOR ENG. CO.	3 CYL. TRIPLE 19"X 32"X 56"X36 1400 3 WATER TUBE	
LAGUNITAS — NORTHWESTERN PACIFIC NORTH SHORE R. R.	WOOD STERN WHEEL	279'-9" 36'-8" 767	JOHN. DICKIE 1903 RISDON IRON WORKS —	POPET VALVE 18" X 72" 400 2 RETURN TUBE	
LAKE TAHOE — S. P. G. G. FERRY SOUTHERN PACIFIC	STEEL SINGLE SCREW	251'-0" R 46'-3" R 19'-2" 2468	MOORE D. D. CO. 1927 NEW LONDON S.B. & E. AND WESTINGHOUSE	4 DIESEL 2 ELECT. MOTORS 1250 —	RENAMED ILLAHEE PUGET SOUND NAVIGATION CO.
MARIN EX-REQUA NORTHWESTERN PACIFIC	WOOD SINGLE END SINGLE SCREW	97'-0" 18'-6" 101	— 1909 STANDARD GAS ENG.CO. —	1-6 CYL. GASOLINE — 130 —	
MELROSE — SOUTHERN PACIFIC	WOOD SIDE WHEEL	294'-0" 43'-0" R 17'-10" 2662	— 1908 — —	2 INCLINED 23½" X 38½" X 96" 1040 —	
MENDOCINO — S. P. G. G. FERRY NORTHWESTERN PACIFIC	STEEL SINGLE SCREW	251'-0" R 46'-3" R 19'-2" 2467	UNION IRON WORKS 1927 NEW LONDON S.B. & E. AND GENERAL ELECTRIC	4 DEISEL 2 ELECT. MOTORS 1250 —	RENAMED NISQUALLY PUGET SOUND NAV. CO.
MONTICELLO — MONTICELLO S. S. CO.	WOOD SINGLE SCREW	126'-0" R 22'-0" R 8'-0" 227	E. SORENSON 1892 —	3 CYL. TRIPLE 12" X 18" X 24" X 14" —	
NAPA VALLEY — S. P. G. G. FERRY MONTICELLO S. S. CO.	STEEL SINGLE SCREW	231'-2" R 62'-5" 15'-3" 2189	UNION IRON WORKS 1910 UNITED ENGINEERING CO. —	4 CYL. TRIPLE 25¾41¾48¾48¾24¾ 2600 4 SINGLE END	
NEWARK — SOUTHERN PACIFIC SOUTH PACIFIC COAST	WOOD SIDE WHEEL	294'-0" 78'-0" 18'-9" 1783	— 1877 — —	VERT. BEAM 65" X 144" 1400 2 SINGLE END	REBUILT AS SACRAMENTO
OAKLAND CHRYSOPOLIS SOUTHERN PACIFIC CENTRAL PACIFIC	WOOD SIDE WHEEL	283'-0" 72'-6" 17'-1" 1672	— 1875 — —	VERT. BEAM 60" X 144" 1225 2 SINGLE END	
OCEAN WAVE — SANTA FE	WOOD SINGLE END SIDE WHEEL	180'-0" R 29'-0" R 9'-0" 724	— 1891 — —	— — — —	

NAME FORMER NAME OPERATOR	HULL TYPE	LENGTH BREADTH DEPTH GROSS TONS	BUILDER – DATE ENGINE BUILDER BOILER MFG.	TYPE ENGINE SIZE HORSEPOWER TYPE BOILER	REMARKS
PERALTA — KEY SYSTEM	STEEL SINGLE SCREW	256'–0" 68'–0" 21'–0" 2075	MOORE D. D. CO. 1927 WESTINGHOUSE BABCOCK & WILCOX	STEAM TURBINE 2 ELECT. MOTORS 2600 4 WATER TUBE	REBUILT, RENAMED KALAKALA PUGET SOUND NAV. CO.
PIEDMONT — SOUTHERN PACIFIC	WOOD SIDE WHEEL	273'–0" 74'–1" 15'–7" 1854	— 1883 — —	1 CYL. HORIZ. 57" X 168" 1385 2 SINGLE END	
REDWOOD EMPIRE — S. P. G. G. FERRY NORTHWESTERN PACIFIC	STEEL SINGLE SCREW	251'–0" R 46'–3" R 19'–2" 2470	MOORE D. D. CO. 1927 NEW LONDON S. B. & E. AND GENERAL ELECTRIC —	4 DEISEL 2 ELECT. MOTORS 1250 —	RENAMED QUINAULT PUGET SOUND NAV. CO.
RUSSIAN RIVER EX–NEW ORLEANS RICHMOND SAN RAFAEL FERRY S. P. G. G. FERRY	STEEL SINGLE SCREW	234'–0" R 63'–6" 19'–3" 1952	UNION IRON WORKS 1924 BUCKEYE ENGINE CO. DE PERE MFG. CO.	3 CYL. TRIPLE 19"X 32"X 56"X 36" 1400 3 WATER TUBE	
SACRAMENTO EX–NEWARK SOUTHERN PACIFIC	WOOD SIDE WHEEL	295'–0" 78'–0" 18'–9" 2254	SOUTHERN PACIFIC 1923 — —	1 CYL. VERT. BEAM 65" X 144" 1400 2 SINGLE END	
SAN FRANCISCO — KEY SYSTEM	WOOD SINGLE SCREW	180'–0" R 38'–0" R 18'–2" 612	JOHN W. DICKIE 1905 — —	2–2 CYL. COMP. 20" X 42"X 28" 2000 2 WATER TUBE	REBUILT AS GOLDEN DAWN
SAN JOSE — KEY SYSTEM RODEO VALLEJO FERRY	WOOD SINGLE SCREW	175'–5" R 38'–0" R 17'–0" 630	JOHN W. DICKIE 1903 — BABCOCK & WILCOX	3 CYL. TRIPLE 18" X 27" X 42"X48 1200 2 WATER TUBE	RENAMED SONOMA VALLEY
SAN LEANDRO — KEY SYSTEM	STEEL SINGLE SCREW	225'–0" 42'–0" 19'–6" 1653	LOS ANGELES S.B. 1923 GENERAL ELECTRIC BABCOCK & WILCOX	STEAM TURBINE 2 ELECT. MOTORS 1350 2 WATER TUBE	
SAN MATEO — S. P. G. G. FERRY SOUTHERN PACIFIC	STEEL SINGLE SCREW	230'–0" 63'–6" 19'–6" 1782	UNION IRON WORKS 1922 — —	3 CYL. TRIPLE 19"X 32" X 54"X36" 1400 3 WATER TUBE	
SAN PABLO — SANTA FE	STEEL SIDE WHEEL	226'–0" R 64'–6" 16'–0" 1584	UNION IRON WORKS 1900 UNION IRON WORKS —	2 CYL. COMP. 38" X 77" X 66" 2000 4 WATER TUBE	
SAN PEDRO — SANTA FE	STEEL SIDE WHEEL	248'–9" 64'–6" 16'–0" 1720	UNION IRON WORKS 1911 UNION IRON WORKS —	2 CYL. COMP. 38" X 77" X 66" 2000 4 WATER TUBE	SOLD TO KEY SYSTEM, RENAMED TREASURE ISLAND
SAN RAFAEL — NORTH PACIFIC COAST R. R.	WOOD SIDE WHEEL	205'–6" R 32'–0" R 9'–9" 692	— 1877 NORTH RIVER IRON WKS. —	1 CYL. VERT. BEAM — 750 (NOMINAL) 	
SANTA CLARA — SOUTHERN PACIFIC	STEEL SIDE WHEEL	293'–0" 76'–0" 17'–3" 2282	SOUTHERN PACIFIC 1915 SOUTHERN PACIFIC —	2 CYL. COMP. 20" X 40" X 96" 1980 4 WATER TUBE	
SANTA ROSA — S. P. G. G. FERRY NORTHWESTERN PACIFIC	STEEL SINGLE SCREW	251'–0" R 46'–3" R 19'–2" 2470	GENERAL ENG. CO. 1927 NEW LONDON S. B. & E. AND GENERAL ELECTRIC	4 DEISEL 2 ELECT. MOTORS 1250 	RENAMED ENETAI PUGET SOUND NAVIGATION CO.
SAUCELITO — NORTH PACIFIC COAST R. R.	WOOD SIDE WHEEL	205'–0" R 32'–0" R 9'–9" 692	— 1878 NORTH RIVER IRON WKS. —	1 CYL. VERT. BEAM — 750 (NOMINAL) 	
SAUSALITO — NORTHWESTERN PACIFIC NORTH PACIFIC COAST R. R.	WOOD SIDE WHEEL	256'–0" 68'–3" 15'–0" 1766	JOHN W. DICKIE 1894 FULTON IRON WORKS —	1 CYL. VERT. BEAM 56" X 144" 1400 3 DRYBACK	
SEHOME — MONTICELLO S. S. CO.	WOOD SIDE WHEEL REBUILT TWIN SCREW	192'–0" R 37'–0" R — 692	— 1889 — —	— — — —	
SHASTA — S. P. G. G. FERRY SOUTHERN PACIFIC	STEEL SINGLE SCREW	230'–0" 63'–0" 19'–6" 1782	UNION IRON WORKS 1922 — —	3 CYL. TRIPLE 19"X 32" X 54"X36" 1400 3 WATER TUBE	

NAME FORMER NAME OPERATOR	HULL TYPE	LENGTH BREADTH DEPTH GROSS TONS	BUILDER – DATE ENGINE BUILDER BOILER MFG.	TYPE ENGINE SIZE HORSEPOWER TYPE BOILER	REMARKS
SIERRA NEVADA EX- FEATHER RIVER RICHMOND SAN RAFAEL FERRY SOUTHERN PACIFIC	STEEL SINGLE SCREW	218'-0" R 42'-0" R 16'-7" 1578	MOORE & SCOTT 1913 — 	2- 2 CYL. COMP. 20" X 42" X 28" 2500 4 WATER TUBE	
SOLANO SOUTHERN PACIFIC CENTRAL PACIFIC	WOOD SIDE WHEEL	420'-5" 116'-0" 18'-4" 3549	CENTRAL PACIFIC 1879 — —	2-1 CYL. VERT BEAM 60" X 132" 2500 8 SCOTCH MARINE	
SONOMA VALLEY EX - SAN JOSE CITY OF MARTINEZ RICHMOND SAN RAFAEL FERRY	WOOD SINGLE SCREW	175'-5" R 38'-0" R 17'-0" 630	JOHN W. DICKIE 1903 BABCOCK & WILCOX	3 CYL. TRIPLE 18"X 27"X 42"X48" 1200 2 WATER TUBE	
STOCKTON S. P. G. G. FERRY SOUTHERN PACIFIC	STEEL SINGLE SCREW	256'-0" 66'-0" 19'-9" 2467	UNION IRON WORKS 1927 NEW LONDON S.B. & E. AND GENERAL ELECTRIC	4 DEISEL 2 ELECT. MOTORS 1250 —	RENAMED KLICKITAT PUGET SOUND NAV. CO.
SUNOL ADEN BROS.	WOOD STERN WHEEL	135'-0" R 27'-6" R 7'-10" 294	— 1890 — —	— — — —	RENAMED PYRAMID
TAMALPAIS NORTHWESTERN PACIFIC NORTH PACIFIC COAST R. R.	STEEL SIDE WHEEL	245'-0" 64'-6" 16'-0" 1631	UNION IRON WORKS 1901 UNION IRON WORKS UNION IRON WORKS	2 CYL. COMP. 36" X 73" X 62" 2100 2 SCOTCH MARINE	
TELEPHONE WESTERN PACIFIC	WOOD STERN WHEEL	201'-0" — — 632	— 1903 — —	— — — —	
THOROUGHFARE SOUTHERN PACIFIC CENTRAL PACIFIC	WOOD SIDE WHEEL	248'-0" — — 1012	— 1871 — —	— — 400 —	
THOROUGHFARE S. P. G. G. FERRY SOUTHERN PACIFIC	WOOD SIDE WHEEL	294'-0" 77'-0" 16'-9" 2620	SOUTHERN PACIFIC 1912 — —	2 CYL. COMP. 22¼" X 38¾" X 96" 1300 2 SCOTCH MARINE	
TIBURON NORTHWESTERN PACIFIC S. F. & N. P. RY. CO.	WOOD SIDE WHEEL	240'-0" 68'-0" 13'-5" 1284	— 1884 P. DONAHUE WM. CRAMP & SON	1 CYL. VERT. BEAM 50" X 132" 1225 2 DRYBACK	
TRANSIT SOUTHERN PACIFIC CENTRAL PACIFIC	WOOD SIDE WHEEL	338'-0" 75'-0" 17'-6" 1566	— 1876 — —	1 CYL. VERT. BEAM 60" X 132" 1533 2 SINGLE END	
UKIAH NORTHWESTERN PACIFIC S. F. & N. P. RY. CO.	WOOD SIDE WHEEL	291'-0" 78'-6" 14'-2" 2564	S.F. & N.P. RY. CO. 1890 FULTON IRON WORKS SEATTLE D. & C. CO.	1 CYL. VERT. BEAM 65" X 144" 2200 4 DRYBACK	REBUILT & RENAMED EUREKA
VALLEJO MARE ISLAND FERRY	WOOD SIDE WHEEL	123'-3" R 31'-6" R 9'-11" 414	— 1879 — —	1 CYL. INCLINED 22" X 60" 455 1 FIRE BOX BLR.	
YERBA BUENA KEY SYSTEM	WOOD SINGLE SCREW	200'-0" 60'-0" 17'-0" 616	JOHN W. DICKIE 1903 — —	3 CYL. TRIPLE 12"X25" X42"X 27" 1200 2 WATER TUBE	RENAMED HARRY E. SPEAS
YERBA BUENA KEY SYSTEM	STEEL SINGLE SCREW	256'-0" 68'-0" 21'-0" 2075	MOORE D. D. CO. 1927 WESTINGHOUSE BABCOCK & WILCOX	STEAM TURBINE 2 ELECT. MOTORS 2600 4 WATER TUBE	
YOSEMITE S. P. G. G. FERRY SOUTHERN PACIFIC	STEEL SINGLE SCREW	230'-0" 63'-6" 19'-6" 1782	UNION IRON WORKS 1923 — —	3 CYL. TRIPLE 19"X 32"X 54"X36" 1400 3 WATER TUBE	SENT TO SOUTH AMERICA RENAMED ARGENTINA

NOTE: ALL DIMENSIONS FOLLOWED BY LETTER "R" ARE REGISTERED DIMENSIONS ONLY.
WHERE DATA WAS UNOBTAINABLE, FERRYBOATS AND PARTICULARS OMITTED.

GASOLINE CAR FERRY

RAMON SACRAMENTO NORTHERN RY.	WOOD SCREW	202'-8" R 39'-11" R 8'- 4" 775	OAKLAND, ANTIOCH & EASTERN RY. 1914 — —	GASOLINE — 500 —	

BIBLIOGRAPHY

Bay Memories (Southern Pacific Company, San Francisco, 1940).

Bonanza Railroads by Gilbert H. Kneiss (Stanford University Press, Stanford University, 1941).

From Shore to Shore: The Key Route. Edited by Vernon Sappers, (Peralta Associates, Oakland, 1948).

Golden Gate: The Story of San Francisco Harbor. By Felix Reisenberg (Alfred A. Knopf, New York, 1940).

Historical Transaction, The Society of Naval Architects and Marine Engineers. 1943.

History of Marin County (Alley Bowen & Company, New York, 1880).

Minutes, Sausalito Land & Ferry Company: 1869 to 1874.

Official Files, Monticello Steamship Company (C. Ferry Hatch, Vallejo, 1927).

Official Files, Southern Pacific - Golden Gate Ferries, Ltd.

Oil Lamps & Iron Ponies. By Frederic Shaw, Clement Fisher, Jr., and George Harlan (Bay Books, Limited, San Francisco, 1949).

Pacific Marine Review. Issues of 1905 to 1950 (San Francisco, 1950).

Paddle Wheel Days in California. By Jerry MacMullen (Stanford University Press, Stanford University, 1944).

Personal Recollections of Raymond H. Clarke, captain, retired, Richmond - San Rafael Ferry & Transportation Company.

Recollections of a Tule Sailor: Captain John Leale. By Marion Leale (George Fields, San Francisco, 1939).

Redwood Empire Review. Various issues (Northwestern Pacific Railroad).

"Saga of the Ferries." By George H. Harlan (*Sausalito News,* Sausalito, 1941).

San Francisco Chronicle. Issues of 1880 to 1950 (San Francisco).

San Francisco Is Your Home. By Samuel Dickson (Stanford University Press, Stanford University, 1947).

Santa Fe, The Railroad That Built an Empire. By James Marshall (Random House, New York, 1945).

Seventy-Five Years of Progress. By Earle Heath (Southern Pacific Company, 1945).

Ships of the Redwood Coast. By Jerry MacMullen (Stanford University Press, Stanford University, 1946).

Some Considerations in Design of Ferryboats. By Charles F. Gross and Charles Green (The Transactions of the Society of Naval Architects and Marine Engineers, 1926).

Southern Pacific Bulletin, "Fifty Years of Achievement" (Southern Pacific Company, San Francisco, 1950).

The Record of American Shipping (American Bureau of Shipping, New York. Volumes of 1885 to 1950).

Virginia & Truckee, A Story of Virginia City and Comstock Times. By Lucius Beebe and Charles Clegg (Grahame Hardy, Oakland, 1949).

INDEX

The type in which this book is set is Linotype Baskerville, noted for its beauty and clarity. Typography and lithography were by El Camino Press, Salinas, California, and binding by the West Trade Bindery, Redwood City, California